THE PASSING OF THE STORM

AND OTHER POEMS

Also from Westphalia Press

westphaliapress.org

The Passing
of the
Storm

---

and Other Poems

by Alfred Castner King

WESTPHALIA PRESS
An imprint of Policy Studies Organization

The Passing of the Storm and Other Poems
All Rights Reserved © 2016 by Policy Studies Organization

Westphalia Press
An imprint of Policy Studies Organization
1527 New Hampshire Ave., NW
Washington, D.C. 20036
info@ipsonet.org

ISBN-13: 978-1-63391-373-8
ISBN-10: 1-63391-373-2

Cover design by Taillefer Long at Illuminated Stories:
www.illuminatedstories.com

Daniel Gutierrez-Sandoval, Executive Director
PSO and Westphalia Press

Updated material and comments on this edition
can be found at the Westphalia Press website:
www.westphaliapress.org

The Passing of the Storm

AND OTHER POEMS

BY

ALFRED CASTNER KING

NEW YORK   CHICAGO   TORONTO

Fleming H. Revell Company

LONDON   AND   EDINBURGH

DEDICATION

PREFACE

Oh that my words were now written !
Oh that they were inscribed in a book !—Job xix, 23.

Books have, from time immemorial, been the conservators of human wisdom, the repositories of information, the mentors of youth and adolescence, the counsellors of manhood, the comfort and companionship of age.

The experience of an individual, school or era, when committed to book form, becomes the common property of all succeeding time, and the accumulated knowledge of the past, transmitted from generation to generation, through the medium of books, may with justice be regarded as the most valuable of human heritages.

But they have not always been unmixed blessings; they have both led and misled; they have elucidated, yet have mystified.

They have dissipated the shadows of ignorance and superstition, but in some instances have confused and obscured the searchlight of truth. In the economy of human affairs, books have been factors of no small importance. They have proved the most potent expositors of iniquitous systems, and when properly directed against crying evils have accomplished speedy reforms. They have precipitated wars, incited revolts and seditions in the cause of progress, yet have intensified prejudice, political, religious and racial. With silent eloquence, they have cried out against the wrongs of those who had none to plead their cause, while in other cases, their influence has tended to perpetuate existing abuses. In some instances they have taught men to be content with servitude, in others have ignited the beacon fires of liberty. Though they are usually found enlisted under the banners of justice, yet no cause has ever been so unworthy, and no institution so unholy, that books have not been written in their defence. In verity, they have sown both wheat and tares.

Books have been written on every conceivable subject, under all conditions, by all sorts of writers, and from an endless variety of motives. The recompense of those who have written them has been equally various. Some have been apotheosized and worshipped, others have been the recipients of orders and decorations of honor at the hands of kings and potentates, while others have received the ovations of admiring multitudes. Some have anonymously contributed their mite toward the enrichment of literature, others have appeared, from whence we know not, and after placing their offerings upon the altars of poesy and art have departed unrewarded into the shadows of obscurity, leaving as footprints innumerable quotations which have become proverbial. Some, as the bards and minnesingers of old who in mediæval castles ate their bread by the sufferance of the feudal lords and barons, have in more recent years been dependent upon the bounty of some munificent, and usually titled patron, to whom they, as a matter of policy, dedicated their strains and panegyrics, consequently wielding mercenary pens. Some who have presumed to write in a manner displeasing to those who sat in high places have met with vilification, exile, imprisonment, decapitation, and have not been strangers to the pillory. Criticism and ridicule are the patent rewards of incipient authorship, while want, neglect and starvation have terminated the career of more than one name afterwards great in the world of letters.

Aside from motives common to all who with reverent steps humbly strive to follow where the great lights of poesy have led, the author of these unpretentious pages has been actuated by a desire to portray, in his correct light, a very frequently misrepresented character, viz.: the pioneer prospector. It has long been customary for writers of western fiction to picture this character as a large-hearted but rough and untutored individual, expressing himself in a vernacular consisting of equal parts of slang, profanity and questionable grammar, possessing no ambitions above the card table or the strong waters which cause all men to err who drink them. An intimate acquaintance with this class, extending from the years of infancy to middle age, convinces the writer that the common description is manifestly unjust and misleading.

The men who flocked to the early gold excitements, and who subsequently prospected the western mountain ranges for their hidden wealth, were the cream of American and European manhood; men possessed of more than ordinary endowments of intellect, education and physique, while their industry, bravery and hardihood have never been questioned.

Proof of this exists in the names which have lingered behind them as a matter of record, for it was the prospector who christened the mountains, gulches and mining locations of the west. A cursory perusal of the maps of mineral surveys in any western mining district, will reveal in abundance such names as Hector, Ajax, Golden Fleece, Atlas, Pegasus, etc.; indicating that those who applied them were, if not college graduates, men not unfamiliar with the classics. The use of such names as Cleopatra, Crusader or Magna Charta, by a prospector unversed in history, would naturally be unexpected. One without knowledge of literature would hardly grace his location stakes with such names as Dante, Hamlet or Mephistopheles, while one entirely unlettered could not by chance hit upon such names as Pandora, Medusa or Sesostris.

Of the pioneer prospectors but few remain; many have fallen asleep, others tiring of the privation and uncertainty incident to a miner's life, are pursuing other vocations, while many have become prosperous ranch and cattle-men and may now be found in almost any western valley. A few, a very few in comparison with the less fortunate majority, acquiring a competence, removed to other localities, and in not a few instances, have become conspicuous figures in the world of business, politics and finance.

In the mountainous districts of the west, you may still occasionally see a veteran prospector of the old school, living the life of a hermit in his log cabin, situated in some picturesque park or gulch, near his, sometimes valuable but more frequently worthless, mining locations. There he lives winter and summer, his only companion a cat or dog; the ambitions of his youth still unrealized, but at three score and ten, hopeful and expectant. His bent form, white hair, and venerable bearing impress you strangely at first, but it is only when you overcome the reticence peculiar to those who have long dwelt in solitude, and engage him in conversation, that his mental status becomes apparent. To your surprise you discover that he can converse entertainingly on any subject, from the Mosaic dispensation, to the latest inventions in the world of mechanism. You may find him to be, not only a Shakspearean scholar, but a deep student of that volume which, whether considered from a sacred or secular point of view, stands pre-eminently forth as the Book of Books. You may find him able to translate Homer, or Virgil, and that the masterpieces of literature are as familiar to him as his own cabin walls. A glimpse at the interior of his cabin discloses an ample stock of newspapers and magazines, while books are not strangers. There is something pathetic about his loneliness; you leave him with the feeling that society has been the loser by his voluntary banishment, and are reminded of Gray's immortal lines:

> "Full many a gem of purest ray serene,
> The dark unfathomed caves of ocean bear;
> Full many a flower is born to blush unseen,
> And waste its sweetness on the desert air."

You speculate upon the story of his life, for you feel that it has a secret, if not a tragedy, connected with it, into which you may not probe. You ask yourself the question, "Has not his life been wasted?" and if he alone is to be considered, there is none but an affirmative answer. But his life has not been barren of results. He has been a contributory factor in the upbuilding of an empire, for he is one of the class who laid the foundations of western prosperity.

These men came west for various reasons, some actuated by the spirit of adventure, some to acquire fortunes or to retrieve vanished ones, others possibly to outlive the stigma of youthful mistakes. In the lives of many of them are sealed chapters. It is with such that these pages have to do.

ALFRED CASTNER KING.

OURAY, COLO., 1907.

CONTENTS

---

14 *Contents*

LIST OF ILLUSTRATIONS

Facing Page

LIST OF ILLUSTRATIONS

The Passing of the Storm

I. THE STORM

Reflecting, in their crystal snows,
The glittering jewels of the night,
The mountains lay in calm repose
Slumbering 'neath their robes of white.

The stars grew dim,—a film instead,
The twinkling heavens overspread,
Through which their eyes essayed to peer,
Each moment less distinct and clear,
Till, when the stellar beacons failed,
A darkness unrelieved, prevailed.

Out of the ambient depths of gloom,
Bereft of its accustomed bloom,
Came day-break, comfortless and gray.
Sped the nocturnal shades away,
Unveiling, with their winged retreat,
A twilight sad and incomplete.
Reluctantly, as dawn aspired,
The shadows lingered, then retired
As vanquished armies often yield
Upon a well-contested field,

And sullenly retrace their course
Before an overwhelming force.

Within the east no purple light
Proclaimed the passing of the night;
No crimson blush appeared to warn
The landscape of returning morn.
Discarding all the gorgeous dyes,
Wherewith the sunset tints the skies,
And mingling with the azure blue,
The warp and woof of sober hue;
The fairies of the air, I wist,
Had spun a silvery web of mist,
Whose texture, ominous and gray,
Obscured the glories of the day.

Such was the dreary winter's day,
Which dawned with dull and leaden sky;
No cheerful penetrating ray
Flashed from the sun's resplendent eye.
In vain, through rift and orifice,
He strove with radiant beam to kiss
Each mountain peak and dizzy height,
Apparelled in their garbs of white,
And crown each brow, so bleak and cold,
With burnished diadem of gold.

Ascending in aërial flight,
The wheel of fire did not appear,
To dissipate the fogs of night

And clarify the atmosphere.
Seeking with fervent ray and fierce,
The canopy of cloud to pierce,
The orb of day, stripped of his flame,
A circle, ill-defined, became,
As through the ever-thickening haze,
His feeble outline met the gaze.
This faded till his glowing face
Left no suggestive spot or trace,
No corollary on the pall
Which settled and pervaded all.

As stormy cowls their summits hid,
In turret, tower and pyramid,
Of stately and majestic mien,
Was nature's architecture seen.
From yawning chasm and abyss,
Rose minaret and precipice,
Carved by the tireless hand of time,
In forms fantastic, yet sublime,
While spires impregnable and high,
Were profiled on the lowering sky.

Exceeding the tremendous height
Of brother peaks, on left and right,
In his commanding station placed,
The giant of the rocky waste
With awe-inspiring aspect stood,
The sentry of the solitude,
Guarding the mountainous expanse
With his imposing battlements.

In rock-ribbed armor panoplied,
With rugged walls on every side,
Beseamed with countless scars and rents,
From combat with the elements,
He towered with mute and massive form,
A challenge to the gathering storm.

This overshadowing mountain peak
In solemn silence seemed to speak
A prophecy of arctic doom;
As in his frigid splendor dressed,
He reared aloft his frozen crest,
Surmounted by a snowy plume.
His wrinkled and forbidding brow
A sombre shadow seemed to throw
O'er other crags as wild and stern,
Which frowned defiance in return.

The wind, lugubrious and sad,
In doleful accents, soft and low,
Mourned through the dismal forests, clad
In weird habiliments of snow,
As if, forsooth, the sylvan ghosts
Had mobilized in pallid hosts,
To haunt their rugged solitudes,
The spectres of departed woods.
And with uninterrupted flow
The streamlet, underneath the snow,
Answered the wind's despondent moan
With plaint of gurgling monotone;

Or, locked in winter's stern embrace,
No longer trickled in its bed,
But found a frigid resting place
In stationary ice, instead.
The crystal snowflakes gently fell,
Enrobing mountain, plain and dell,
In mantle spotless and complete,
As nature in her winding sheet.
Layer upon layer fell fast and deep
Till every cliff, abrupt and steep,
Was crowned with coronal of white.
Capricious gusts, which whirl and sift,
Built comb and overhanging drift,
From feathery flakes so soft and light.

More thickly flew the snow and fast;
The wind developed and the blast
Soon churned the tempest, till the air
Seemed but a white and whirling glare,
Through which the penetrating eye
No shape nor contour might descry.

The poor belated traveller,
Who braved the rigor of that day,
Might thank his bright protecting star,—
If orbs of pure celestial ray,
Far in the scintillating skies,
Preside o'er human destinies,—
That he, bewildered and distressed,
Had warded off exhaustion's rest,

And in that maze of pine and fir
Escaped an icy sepulchre.

When driving snows accumulate,
They yield to the tremendous weight.
And down the mountain's rugged sides
The mass with great momentum slides,
Cleaving the fragile spruce and pine,
Which stand in its ill-fated line,
As bearded grain, mature and lithe,
Goes down before the reaper's scythe.
Or, when the cyclone's baleful force,
In flood of atmospheric wrath,
Pursues its devastating course,
Leaving but ruin in its path;
Despoiling in a moment's span
The most exalted works of man;
Or waters, suddenly set free,
When some black thunder cloud is rent,
Rush down a wild declivity
With irresistible descent,
Depositing on every hand
A layer of sediment and sand;
With swift and spoliating flow,
Uprooting many a noble tree,
To strew the desert wastes below
With scattered drift-wood and debris;
Such is the dreadful avalanche,
Which rends the forest, root and branch.

From dangers in such varied form,
And the discomforts of the storm,
Small wonder 'twas the mountaineer
Left not his fireside's ruddy cheer;
But from behind the bolted door
Discerned the tempest's strident roar,
Or heard the pendent icicle,
Which, from the eaves, in fragments fell,
As some more formidable blast
In paroxysmal fury passed.
It shook with intermittent throes,
Of boisterous, spasmodic power,
A most substantial hut, which rose,
As summer breeze sways grass or flower
And e'en the dull immobile ground
Trembled in sympathy profound.

Such was the fury of the storm,
As if the crystal flakes had met
With militating hosts, to swarm
In siege about its parapet.

When every rampant onslaught failed,
The blast in wanton frenzy wailed.
As if with unspent rage the wind
Felt much disgruntled and chagrined,
And though of nugatory force,
Could vent its spleen with accents hoarse.
As some beleaguered tower of old
Besieged by warriors stern and bold,

Who dashed against its walls of stone,
Which were not swayed nor overthrown;
As vicious strokes delivered well,
Innocuous and futile fell.
Then watched the walls withstand the strain,
And cursed and gnashed their teeth in vain.

Beneath a massive pinnacle,
Whose weird, forbidding shadows fell,
And gulch and forest overcast
With mantle ominous and vast,
Nestling amid the spruce and pine,
Which fringe the edge of timberline,
This miner's cabin, quaint and rude,
From the surrounding forest hewed,
With primitive, yet stable form,
Withstood the onslaught of the storm,
And at the entrance of a dell
Stood as a rustic sentinel.

Beneath a pine's protecting skirt,
It reared its modest roof of poles,
Laid close, then overlaid with dirt,
To cover up the cracks and holes;
The intervals between the logs
Were daubed with mud from mountain bogs.
The ground did service as a floor
In this, as many huts before;
So beaten down beneath the tread,
It more resembled tile instead.

The plastic clay, compressed and sleek,
Was level and as hard as brick.
Protruding boulders, smooth and bare,
Exposed their faces here and there;
And with their surfaces displayed,
A primitive mosaic made.
And, terminating in a stack,
Some feet above the cabin's roof,
The fireplace, comfortless and black,
Arose the dingy form uncouth.
This object of depressing gloom,
Built in the corner of the room,
When filled with lurid tongues of flame,
A cheerful cynosure became.

The furnishings within were crude;
A table fastened to the wall
Had been with some exertion hewed
From aspen timbers straight and tall,
And was, in lieu of table legs,
Supported by protruding pegs.
A cracker box, with shelves inside,
The leading corner occupied,
And made an ample cupboard there,
Where tin supplanted chinaware.
A frying pan, which from a nail
Suspended, dripped a greasy trail.
Framed from the hemlock's poles and boughs,
The rustic bunks within the house

Were not elaborate affairs;
While boxes filled the place of chairs.

Tacked on the unpretentious wall
Were advertisements, great and small,
While lithograph and crayon scenes,
Clipped from the standard magazines,
Comprised a mimic gallery,
Which broke the wall's monotony.
No carpets were upon that floor,
But at the bottom of the door
The rug, against its yawning crack,
Consisted of a gunny-sack.
Nor was there lock upon that door,
The guardian of sordid pelf;
The traveller, distressed and sore,
Might enter there and help himself.

Within this weather-beaten hut
Of logs, by many a tempest tried,
With doors and windows closely shut,
To keep the genial warmth inside;
A group of hardy mountaineers,
Blockaded by the winter's snow,
Sat by the fireside's ruddy glow.
Some old, and old beyond their years,
As disappointments, toil and strife,
Which constitute the miner's life,
Must operate with process sure,
Toward age, unduly premature;

For years, in stern privation spent,
Are traced in seam and lineament,
Which gives the patriarchal face
Its rugged dignity and grace.

Although by fond illusions led,
Through phantasies of empty air,
Which mark an ultimate despair,
The miner still sees hope ahead.
The prospector could never cope
With dangers and realities,
But for the visionary hope
Which both deceives and mollifies,
Alluring him with siren song
Her vague uncertain paths along.

Yet some, this stalwart group among,
Were adolescent,—even young.
For hearts, which youthful breasts conceal,
Oft burn with energetic zeal,
To ope, with labor's patient key,
The mountain's hidden treasury.

Most furiously it blew and snowed,
Most cheerily the firelight glowed,
And as the forkèd tongues of flame,
In fierce combustion, writhed and burned,
Nor moment's space remained the same,
The conversation swayed and turned.

For tales were told of avalanche,
Of army scenes, of mine and ranch,
Of wily politician's snares,
Of gold excitements, smallpox scares,
Of England's debt and grizzly bears.

When all but three their stories told
Of tropic heat, or arctic cold,
The conversation dragged at length,
An interim for future strength.
Outspoke a voice: "Let Uncle Jim
Some past experience relate,
For Fate has kindly granted him,
At least, diversity of fate."

II. A CHAPTER FROM AN OLD MAN'S LIFE

As ample wreaths of curling smoke
From his time-honored meerschaum broke,
A kindly-faced, gray-bearded man
Rose up and sadly thus began,—
"You ask a tale,—well, I'll express
The reason why in manhood's prime
I left a more congenial clime
And sought this rugged wilderness."
But, gentle reader, don't expect
A tale in mongrel dialect,
For "Uncle Jim," or James T. Hale,
Who lived as anchorite or monk,
Once led the senior class at Yale,

And had his sheepskin in his trunk.
There, while the crackling flames leaped high,
And serpentine gyrations played
Around the logs of hemlock, dry,
And with the tempest seethed and swayed,
As curled the drowsy wreaths of smoke
Above his pipe, the old man spoke:

" 'Twas on a day about like this,
When, fresh from youthful haunts and scenes,
I first beheld yon precipice,
And sought these gulches and ravines,
To pan, despite the frost and cold,
For shining particles of gold;
And hewed the rocker and the sluice
From out the native pine and spruce.
Arrayed in nature's pristine dress
This was indeed a wilderness.
Nor eye of eagle ever viewed
A more forbidding solitude,
Nor prospect more completely drear
Confronted hardy pioneer.

Why came I here? My simple tale
Goes back to a New England vale.
It is, though simple tale it be,
A life's unwritten tragedy:
A story, with few incidents,
But many years of penitence.

As one, for some foul crime pursued,
Doth flee, in frenzy rash and blind
To wilderness or solitude,
I fled, to leave my past behind.

I loved a maid, both fair and true,
Just where, it matters not, nor who.
For forty years, with silent tread,
Have silvered many a raven head,
Since on her wealth of auburn hair
The moonlight shimmered, soft and **fair,**
As where the pine and hemlock stood
And sighed in answer to the breeze,
With but the stars as witnesses,
Our troth was plighted in the wood;
A simple rustic tale in truth,
Of love and sentimental youth.

Love is the subtle mystery,
The charm, the esoteric spell,
Which lures the seraph from on High.
To leave the Throne of Light,—for Hell,—
And with resistless shackles binds,
In viewless thrall, the captive minds.
For who can fathom love's caprice,
Supplant her fervid wars with peace,
And passion's ardent flame command?
Or who presume to understand
And read with cabalistic art
The hieroglyphics of the heart?

Nor eye of regent, skilled to rule,
Nor sage from earth's profoundest school,
Nor erudite philosophy
On wisdom's heights, pretend to see
The fervent secrets of the breast,
Which rankle mute and unexpressed.
Nor the angelic hosts above
In their exuberance of love,
Nor demons from the pit can span
The depths of woman's love for man.
And men, of love's sweet flame bereft,
Have but the brutal instincts left.

She, too, my youthful love returned,
Each breast with throb responsive yearned,
The oracles of passion sweet,
All augured happiness complete.
But, ere the nuptial knot was bound,
A whispered rumor crept around,
A whispered rumor, such as rise
From nothing to colossal size;
Though none their origin can trace,
Nor ferret out the starting place,
Which start sometimes, in idle jest,
When knowing looks imply the rest.
The lightest rumor, or the worst,
May be discredited at first,
But oft repeated and received
Is soon unconsciously believed.
Though inconsistent and abstract,

Fanned by insinuating tongues,
Imaginary faults and wrongs
Soon gain the currency of fact.
The purest acts are misconstrued
By the lascivious and lewd,
And envy loves to lie in wait
With fangs imbrued in venomed hate.
This slander, born of jealousy,
Was told as solemn truth to me,
By tongues I deemed immaculate.

Alas! that shafts from falsehood's bow
Should undetected cleave the air,
Or wanton hands in malice sow
The tares of discord and despair.
For every seed of falsehood sown
Brings forth a harvest of its own,
And ears, most ready to believe,
Are difficult to undeceive.
Alas! that shafts from falsehood's tongue
Should fall suspicious ears among,
And be received, and nursed, forsooth,
As arrows of unblemished truth:
Maligning spotless innocence,
With grave impeachments of offence.
Their crime, of heinous crimes the worst,
With multiplied damnation cursed,
Who, lost to every sense of shame,
Assassinate a woman's name.

For such, with trumped-up calumnies,
Would drag an angel from the skies,
And stain its vestal robes of white
With slander's sable hues of night,
Holding to ridicule and shame
The ruins of a once fair name.

Who so, from slander's chalice sips,
May greet you with a friendly kiss,
Nor may the foul, envenomed lips
Betray the adder's sting and hiss.
The fairest flowrets of the field
The rankest poisons often yield,
And falsehood loves to hide her tooth
'Neath the habiliments of truth.
This scandal, venomous and vile,
Had no foundation but a smile,
But on it wagging tongues had built
A massive pyramid of guilt.

In evil hour, I, too, believed
For fabrications more absurd
Than the aspersions I had heard
Have wiser ears than mine deceived.
I fought suspicion, vainly tried
To cast each rising doubt aside.
But he who lists to tales of ill
Believes in part, despite his will.
Then in my face, as in a book,
She read one sad distrustful look,

A look of pity, yet of doubt,
For silence cries most loudly out,
And who can smile with visage bright
To shield misgivings black as night?

Unhappy trait that in us lies!
We doubt the verdict of our eyes;
We doubt each faculty and sense,
Yet credit sham and false pretence.
We question Truth, and much prefer
To list to Falsehood, than to her:
And that, which most substantial seems,
We doubt, yet place our faith in dreams.
We doubt the pearl of purest white,
We doubt the diamond clear and bright,
And yet accept the base and flawed,
Yes, revel in all forms of fraud.

That moment's lack of confidence,
The shadow of remote offence,
Cost each the sweetest joys of life,
Cost her a husband, me a wife.

Ere yet that month its course had spent,
In time's continuous descent,
Her race had been forever hid
Beneath the sod and coffin lid.
Then slanderous tongues forgot their lies,
And wagged in glowing eulogies.

Though tears, the pearls of sorrow be,
And many o'er her grave were shed,
Mine was a tearless agony,
A deeper, dry-eyed grief instead.

That rumor, void of fact or proof,
Too late betrayed the cloven hoof.
Too late, alas! 'twas given me
To recognize its falsity.

Within a rural burial place,
A rude, though quaint, necropolis,
Where, through the growth of hemlock trees,
Is borne the requiem of the breeze;
Where stand the funeral pines as plumes,
Above the scattered graves and tombs,
And sigh, with drooping branches spread,
In sylvan dirges for the dead;
Beneath a fir tree's sombre shade,
My last adieu to her was made.

Close by the slab of graven stone,
Which marks her place of silent rest,
I knelt at midnight, and alone,
Then rose and started for the West."

.   .   .   .

The wind in temporary lull,
Had dwindled to a plaintive moan;
As if in mournful monotone,
Her cup of anguish being full,

Sad nature's fountain-heads of bale
Had overflowed with plaint and wail.
In palpitating throbs of woe,
It now arose and whirled the snow
With triple energy renewed,
Filling the dismal solitude
With woeful shriekings of despair,
As demon orgies in the air,
And culminated in a roar
More violent than aught before.

.   .   .   .

At length another timely lull
Made human voices audible.
As Uncle Jim resumed his seat,
A voice cried out for Russian Pete.

.   .   .   .

III. THE PRISONER

Of Russian Pete but little had been known,
He liked to read and be so much alone;
No more his close associates could tell,
Save that he spoke the English language well.
About this stranger with the clever tongue,
An air of mystery and sadness clung.
His name, so long and unpronounceable,
Which none could frame, much less presume to spell,
Waiving abridgment, partial or complete,
Was, by the boys, transformed to "Russian Pete."

Now Russian Pete was tall and strong of limb,
Nor more than half as old as Uncle Jim,
Of noble stature and commanding brow,
With knees which in no genuflections bow.
His face was sad, the index of a breast
Where memory's fires were raging unsuppressed.
With eyes which search in closest scrutiny,
Nor yet offend the object they would see.
One, who from feature, act and equipoise,
Had known life's sorrows better than its joys.
A man whom you would notice in the street,
And know the second time if you should meet.

This man of mystery and intellect
Arose, and stood in manhood's poise erect.
In tone of voice so musical and clear
It might have charmed the most exacting ear,
And wealth of language few can hope to reach,
Nor trace of foreign accent in his speech,
He forthwith spake: "My simple tale shall be,
Not one of love, but dire captivity.
Like Uncle Jim's, however, it contains
The cause why I forsook my native plains.
No tender web of sentiment, but one
By treachery and machination spun.

Across the sea, in distant realms afar,
In the remote dominions of the Czar,
Past where the Dnieper rolls his murky flood,
Surcharged with fertilizing silt and mud,

Past the dark forests and productive plains,
Which he with many a tributary drains;
Within that city whose inhabitants,
With flaming torch, withstood the arms of France,
Preferring ruin to the victor's boast,
Or occupation by an alien host.
Fair Moscow, which became a funeral pyre,
And perished in her self-ignited fire,
That her invaders, chilled by snow and sleet,
Might sink in irretrievable defeat.
A few years since, the date concerns us not,
A minor detail readily forgot,
Beneath the shadow of her noblest spire,
There dwelt two students, children of one sire.

With prospects fair at manhood's budding edge,
In caste esteemed of no base parentage;
Two students, versed in languages, and planned
For consul service in a distant land,
As foreign usages are studied most,
When one aspires to diplomatic post.
Thus eagerly, did we acquire the tongue
Of you, whom I address and live among.
With lucubrations diligent, we sought
Our ways up varied avenues of thought,
Until by prejudice no longer bound,
We stood at last upon dissenting ground;
Or wavered, where reluctant doubts confuse,
In that strange zone of ruminating views,

Where progress and established custom meet;
Yes, crossed its boundaries with reckless feet.

In that stern Empire, on disruption's brink,
Some things you may,—and some you may not,—
    think;
Express yourself, and instantly disgraced,
Your steps may point toward a Siberian waste;
Your substance confiscated by a court
Where equity is but a theme for sport;
Extol your theories, proffer your advice,
And chains or banishment may be the price.

For despot hands, since might's initial sway,
Have fashioned chains for worthier hands than they;
And oftentimes beneath the tyrant's heel
Are crushed the lives which strive for human weal;
Who dare to hold the gonfalon aloft
For human rights and progress, yes, how oft
Since Cain that fratricidal murder wrought,
Have death and durance been the price of thought!

He who espouses radical reform
Invites upon his head the gathering storm;
Each forward step from Custom's hackneyed school,
Draws forth the floods of scorn and ridicule;
Witness the dungeon, guillotine and rack,
Chains for the feet and scourges for the back;
Bestrewn with insult, diatribe and cuff,
The pathway of reform was ever rough;

And when reforms, as tidal waves have come,
The foremost breakers dash to martyrdom.

Perhaps, in youth's enthusiastic heat
We may have been a little indiscreet,
When we, thus inexperienced and young,
Against oppression dared to raise the tongue.
Perhaps 'twere best to tarnish manhood's brow
With servile adulation, and to bow
With craven salaam and obeisance, down
In sycophantic homage to a crown.
What, though the diadem its blazon rears
Above a population's groans and tears!
What, though the paths of tyranny be strew'd
With suspirations of the multitude!
If one but bask within the regal smile,
Why strive against injustice, fraud and guile?
Or, why enlist the sympathetic pen,
Though thrones may crush the liberties of men?

One inadvertent hour, some chance remark
Was misconstrued with application dark;
For little is required as an excuse
When private ends are furthered by abuse;
Suspicion's tunes are played with greatest ease,
When jealousy manipulates the keys.
What followed, it were wearisome to tell,
Save that we found ourselves within a cell,
Charged with sedition and conspiracy,
By those more likely to conspire than we.

Three days were we, in custody detained,
In stern abeyance formally constrained.
Within a court, where no protesting word
From prisoner or counsel may be heard;
A court, where no forensic eloquence
May quash the allegations of offence;
Our doom was sealed, by a capricious judge
Who thereby satisfied a family grudge.

The sentence passed, the stalwart Cossack guard
Straightway transferred us to a prison yard.
There parted we, before its grated door;
They dragged him in,—and he was seen no more.

Another door, with dull metallic sound
Was closed, and I was hurried underground,
Through labyrinth of passages and halls,
Past dingy arches and protruding walls,
Where gloom perpetual the eye obscures,
Through damp recesses, nooks and apertures,
With foul effluvia and odors filled,
By darkness, dampness and decay distilled.
For noisome vapors float in gaseous waves,
In cavern depths of men-created caves,
And generate in humid warmth or cold
The loathsome mildew and corrupting mould.

At length, through cruel maze of grate and stone,
By paths circuitous and ways unknown,

We reached the cell,—as hideous a den,
As ever held unwilling beasts or men.
And soon with manacles securely bound,
Myself its only occupant I found.
A dungeon, dimly lighted and obscure,
With pools of water, stagnant and impure,
Whose noxious exhalations permeate
The deadened air, which could not circulate;
And laden with malignant slime and ooze,
Upon the walls discharged in baneful dews;
Or else precipitate, with vapory loss,
Enrobed the cruel stones with pendent moss.
And water, foul as e'er offended lip,
Fell from the roof with intermittent drip.
Remote from daylight, dismal and unsunned,
Decompositions stored a teeming fund
Of molecules and organisms strange,
In an invisible but constant change.
As stagnant waters generate a froth,
These, with spontaneous and fungous growth,
Had draped the dungeon's limited expanse
With toadstool, bulb and foul protuberance.
These from the air its milder virtues drank,
Supplanting ichors, venemous and dank,
Whose essence deleterious, the while,
Exudes in savors and miasmas vile.

High on the wall, a double-grated slit
A slender ray of sunshine would admit

On pleasant mornings, when the sky was clear
From leaden fogs and hazy atmosphere.
A ray of sunlight, yes, a welcome ray,
A wholesome beam, but just too far away.
Although I tugged at the remorseless chain
And strove to reach that sunbeam, 'twas in vain;
The lambent gleam which broke into the cell
Alone on toad and savage rodent fell.
In vain I wrenched the manacles, in vain
I sought to rend the cruel gyves in twain,
Strove, with contortions painful and extreme,
To lay my head within this gladsome beam,
Or even touch it with the finger-tip;
In vain,—no galling chain relaxed its grip.

A ray of sunlight just beyond my reach,
Like Tantalus, as ancient classics teach,
When for duplicity and theft immersed,
In rippling waters, doomed to ceaseless thirst,—
For as his parching lips essayed to drink,
The mocking waters would recede, or sink;
Though luscious fruits hung pendent in his sight,
To coax the palate and the appetite,
Whene'er his hand reached forth with eager thrust,
Those selfsame fruits resolved to baleful dust.
That sunbeam, though an aggravation fair,
Still closed the floodgates of complete despair.
As dykes constrain, in distant lowland realms,
The deluge, which engulfs and overwhelms.

With final resource and expedient
And all her vials of expectation spent,
Fate, in her changeable kaleidoscope,
Evolves new turns to reëstablish hope.
That ray of sunshine, as an angel's smile,
Beaming in love amid surroundings vile,
Came, morn by morn, to mitigate and bless;
A benediction in my bitterness.

Time after time, when the approaching night
Had banished every modicum of light,
And clothed each outline with her sable guise,
I watched the greenish glow of reptile eyes,
Nor dared to slumber, till exhaustion's sleep
Benumbed my senses with its stupors deep.
Then, conjured by the witcheries of night,
Came pleasant dreams and visions of delight,
Those iridescent phantasies of air,
Which mock the troubled breast in its despair;
Then waking, the delusive phantoms flown,
A prisoner upon a floor of stone.
My fare was still the captive's mouldy crust,
My chains still reeked with clotted gore and rust,
The rigid shackles still retained their clutch,
And clammy walls repulsed the friendly touch.

Day after day, besmeared with filth and slime,
In foul monotony I passed the time,
Battling with vermin foes, a teeming brood,
Prolific and not easily withstood:

An evil pest, ubiquitous and rife,
In the fecundity of insect life.
In agony of body and of brain,
Each breath a stifling gasp and twinge of pain,
Cursing my fortune, though each fevered curse
Redounding, made my agony the worse;
For fits of anger seldom mollify,
When vacancy reiterates the cry,
Or walls of cold, unsympathetic stone
Respond but hollow echoes of a groan.
Though limbs as free and restless as the wind
Are not to shackles readily resigned,
Complaint, with oath and bitterness replete,
In prisoner is doubly indiscreet.
The imprecation, born of righteous wrath,
Subtracts no obstacle from any path.

Bereft of star or luminary bright,
No night so dark as artificial night;
No glittering constellations kindly throw
Their twinkling beacons o'er the void below;
No satellite with pale invasive beam
Breaks through the darkness awful and extreme;
No comet, through the vast sidereal waste,
Pursues its orbit with unbridled haste;
No silvery moon, through the dissembling shroud,
May shine or burst through orifice of cloud
In mellow radiations, soft and sweet;
Darkness most dense, oppressive and complete.

No friendly voice might penetrate the gloom,
Nor break the silence of that fetid tomb,
With genial converse, which in some degree
Makes men forget their depth of misery.
Silence, most tragic, horrible, profound,
Except the sharp and intermittent sound
Of rodent feet, and noise of creeping things,
The squeak of vampires and their whirr of wings;
Or cries of swift pursuit, or of despair,
Rang out upon the pestilential air,
As ever and anon a dying squeak
Told of the strong prevailing o'er the weak;
For might obtains along the selfsame plan
With ruthless vermin and enlightened man.
Yet man in his dominion absolute,
Removed above the province of the brute,
From social claims and attributes released,
Has little to distinguish from the beast.
With all associative wants denied,
And his gregarious longings unsupplied,
By human comradeship, affection springs
Well up in effluent love for baser things.
For 'neath the polish and embellishments
Of cultivation and intelligence,
There lies a basic bond of sympathy,
For man and beast are friends in misery.
Yes, friends, the most ill-favored shape which squirms
In reptile folds, repulsive snakes and worms,
Soon lose their dread repugnance, one and all,
To solitary man in prison thrall.

Through the long hours of physical distress,
In my extremity of loneliness,
I felt companionship in this abode,
For e'en the vicious rat and sluggish toad.

Thrice sixty days of corporal decay
And mental anguish, slowly wore away;
Thrice sixty nights of filthy durance passed,
Each day and night more hopeless than the last.
My limbs, no longer brawny and alert,
Were famine-wasted, loathsome and inert.
With shaggy beard and matted unkempt hair,
With face no longer rubicund and fair,
Which haggard and emaciated shone,
And through the sallow skin disclosed the bone.
Thus languished nature in enforced decay,
Till hope's last beacon light had burned away.

Though never exculpated from offence,
Time brought conditional deliverance;
A writ of amnesty, the Czar's decree,
Within its gracious scope included me.
Released at last by ukase absolute,
But famished, homeless, sick and destitute.
What followed would be tedious to recite,
The sequel, but the incidents of flight.
Alone, an outcast from my native hearth,
An aimless wanderer upon the earth,
Blown as the desert shifts a grain of sand,
Borne by each wanton gale, from land to land.

A keen observer of the play of life,
Withal a nether factor in its strife.
Watching existence as a game of chess,
Where love, hate, smile, tear, insult and caress
Hold us by turns in various forms of check;
Some sort of yoke is worn by every neck.
Kings, queens and knights, exalted castles see,
Undone by pawns and powers of base degree.
Positions gained at a tremendous cost,
By one false move may be forever lost;
Each studied movement, each strategic course,
Is shaped by contact with opposing force,
And moves which seem fortuitous and blind
Are often those most cunningly designed.
In devious ways we may not understand,
Our steps are ordered by an Unseen Hand.
Proud queens, subservient pawns, with varied rôle,
Are vain components of the wondrous whole;
Life's pantomime, in figures complicate;
Men are but puppets on the wires of fate.

   .   .   .   .

My native land, henceforth no longer mine,
My footsteps, seeking an adopted shrine,
Have found a home, within the mountain West,
Where Truth may preach her gospel unsuppressed."

   .   .   .   .

   .   .   .   .

All eyes were now on Russian Pete,
Who quietly resumed his seat.

At the conclusion of his tale
The wind had risen to a gale,
And mourned as though in sympathy
With human woe and misery.
Or as the winds, for some offence
To man, or his creations done,
Now wailed a frenzied penitence
In anguish-laden orison.
The elements petitioning
The pardon of their stormy king,
E'en as the supplicating cries
Might from the damned in torment rise,
And cleave the palpitating air
With hopeless accents of despair.

.   .   .   .

As Uncle Jim stirred up the fire
With observation taciturn,
All watched the crackling hemlock burn
Till some one called for Dad McGuire.

IV. A SEQUEL OF THE LOST CAUSE

Now, Dad McGuire was old, and bent of form,
Tanned by exposure to the sun and storm;
Of grizzled beard and seam-indented brow,
The furrows traced by Time's remorseless plough;
Hardy and gnarlèd as the mountain oak,
Bent by the hand of Time but still unbroke;
Bowed by the weight of years and labors done,
A man whose course had neared the setting sun;

His face a blending of the calm and sad,
Paternal-looking, so they called him "Dad."

 . . . .

This man, so near his journey's close,
With great deliberation rose,
Coughed once or twice and scratched his nose;
Then, as became a veteran,
Surveyed his hearers and began:
"Since Uncle Jim and Russian Pete
Declared the reasons why their feet
This rugged wilderness have trod,
And left for aye their native sod,
I, too, will recapitulate
That chapter, from my book of fate.

Where Rappahannock's silver stream
Reflects the moon's resplendent beam,
And sheds a mellow lustre o'er
The trees and shrubs that fringe the shore;
Where Nature's lavish hand bestows
The crystal dews and generous showers;
Where lily, hollyhock and rose,
And many-tinted herbs and flowers
Combining, form a floral scene
On background of eternal green;
Where through the solemn night is heard
The warbling plaint of feathered throats,
As whippoorwill and mockingbird
Pour forth their wealth of liquid notes,

While the accompanying breeze
Sighs through the underbrush and trees,
And rippling waters blend their tune,
In salutation to the moon;
Where singing insects, bugs and bees
Mingle their droning harmonies,
With croakings of loquacious frogs
In the adjacent swamps and bogs;
Where from the water, air and ground,
Rises a symphony of sound;
Mid nature's fond environment,
My boyhood's happy hours were spent.

But now, my narrative begins:
I had a brother, we were twins,
Sunburnt and freckled, light of heart,
Resembling each other so
That few could tell the two apart.
We grew, as two twin pines might grow,
Upon the isolated edge
Of some lone precipice or ledge,
That overlooks the vale below;
Remote from every wooded strip,
With but each other's fellowship,
In solitary station placed,
With branches locked and interlaced,
As sworn to cherish and defend
Each other, to the bitter end.

The course of uneventful life
Ran smoothly on, unmarred by strife,

Till childish fancy disappeared,
As manhood's sterner age was neared;
Then in a city's bustling mart,
The cords of fate drew us apart,
Through paths of accident and chance,
Environment and circumstance;
Within their complicated maze,
We reached that parting of the ways,
Where sentiment is nipped by frost,
Where ties of consanguinity
Disrupt, and often disagree,
Or, through indifference are lost.

We happened that eventful spring,
To hold a family gathering,
To reunite each severed tie
So soon to be dissolved for aye.

As famines, with their blight respond,
When some vile genius waves his wand,
And leave a ghastly aftermath
Of bleaching bones to mark their path;
Or demon hands, in foul offence,
Pour out the vials of pestilence,
To reap, with desolating breath,
A harvest of untimely death;
The throes of internecine war
Now rent the nation to its core,
And smote, with decimating hand
The best and bravest of the land,

Estranging, never to amend,
Father from son and friend from friend;
Dissolving many sacred cords
Of love in bitterest enmity.
Lips once replete with friendly words
Now challenged as an enemy;
We, who had never quarrelled before,
Parted in wrath, and met no more.

His firm convictions led him where
A banner floated in the air,
In silken corrugations curled,
The admiration of a world;
Beneath its constellated stars,
Its azure field and crimson bars,
Although no message ever came
To tell his fate, or spread his fame,
I know that 'mid the shot and shell
He served the cause he fought for, well.
For aught I know, his manly form
Went down before some leaden storm,
And lay with mangled flesh and bone
Among the numberless unknown,
Who filled the trenches where they died,
Uncoffined, unidentified.

The voice of duty led me where
The strains of Dixie filled the air,
Where curling smoke in graceful rings
Rose on the evening's silent wings,

And hovering o'er the mist and damp,
Betrayed the presence of the camp.
I pass the story of the war,—
The cause we lost, but struggled for
Through four long years, in southern fens,—
To wiser tongues and abler pens.
Through four long years of tragedy,
I fought, bled, marched and starved with Lee,
Till Appomattox's final day,
I, in a uniform of gray,
Before the cannon's yawning mouth,
Defended my beloved South.

The struggle ending, in complete,
Although most honorable defeat,
Footsore and hungry, broken, sad,
In ragged regimentals clad,
Towards Rappahannock's silver flood,
I plodded homeward through the mud,
To find a desolated home,
The final page in war's red tome.

That day, as I remember well,
The splashing rain in torrents fell;
The pregnant clouds discharged their debt
Of moist, apologetic tears,
As if in passionate regret
For rain withheld in famine years,
And from exuberance of grief
In drizzling penance found relief;

Or, as if tears from unseen eyes
Were wafted downward from the skies,
In tardy expiation for
The carnage of remorseless war;
The sorrow of the elements
For human woe and violence.
The roads which thread the country lanes,
Had turned to sheets of liquid mud,
As if to cover up the stains
Of civil war and human blood.

That evening, as a pall of cloud
Enveloped nature as a shroud,
Bedraggled and dispirited,
My footsteps to the old home led;
Again I stood before the door
I left in wrath, four years before;
But what a change! The vandal torch
Had long devoured the roof and porch;
The gray disintegrating walls
Still swayed and tottered in the air,
Or lay in heaps within its halls,
In melancholy ruin there;
The towering chimney, black and tall,
Stood, as if mourning o'er its fall;
And through the dismal mist and rain,
The windows, void of sash and pane,
Seemed staring at the gathering night,
In wild expression of affright.

The fields my infancy had known,
With briar and weed were overgrown;
The sunlight, heralding the morn,
No longer smiled on waving corn.

I wandered, aimlessly around,
Yet heard not one familiar sound,
No stamp of hoof nor flap of wing,
No low of cow, nor bleat of sheep,
Nor any tame domestic thing;
Silence, most horrible and deep.
No pony whinnied in its stall,
Nor neighed in answer to my call;
No purr of cat, nor bark of dog,
Naught but the croaking of the frog;
No voice of relative or kin,
No father paused and stroked his chin,
Then rushed with recognizing grasp
To hold his son within his clasp;
No mother, with her silvered hair,
Rocked in the same old rocking chair.

First at the ruins, then the ground,
I gazed in turn, mechanically,
Till, startled by a mournful sound,
A piteous and plaintive cry,
I turned, and peering through the storm,
Discerned the outlines of a form,
Bewailing o'er the ruins there
In accents of complete despair.

I knew her voice, and felt her woe,
She was my nurse, poor Aunty Chloe!
Between her sobs disconsolate,
This freed, but ever faithful slave,
Told of my agèd parents' fate,
Then led me to the double grave.

I, who through four long tragic years,
Had never yielded once to tears,
Clasping her hand, so kind and true,
Wept with the rain, and she wept too.

　　.　.　.　.　.　.　.　.

Ere daybreak, with increasing light,
Evolved from disappearing night
The morn, in radiant splendor dressed,
I, too, had started for the West."

　　.　.　.　.　.　.　.　.
　　.　.　.　.　.　.　.　.

Ere the conclusion of the narrative,
Through every crack and cranny of the door
The snow had sifted in, as through a sieve,
And piled in little cones upon the floor.
Without, the raging tempest still assailed;
Within, the fire to glowing coals had failed.
All smoked, and with their eyes on Dad McGuire,
Waited for some one else to build the fire.
Such close attention had his tale received,
It seemed as if 'twas partially believed;
Few of the tales which we enjoy the most
In verity, may that distinction boast.

The dying embers shed their mellow glow
Upon the agèd face of Dad McGuire,
As he swept out the little piles of snow
And laid a hemlock log upon the fire.
Then followed disconnected colloquies
And witticisms in the form of jest;
The joke is always where the miner is,
The form of levity he loves the best,
For cutting truths have thereby been conveyed,
Where delicacy all other forms forbade.

As some fierce gale that bows the gnarlèd oak,
Sinks till it scarcely sways the underbrush,
The laughter, incident to jest and joke,
Subsided to a calm and tranquil hush.
All husbanded their energy and strength
And smoked in silence for a moment's length.

   .   .   .   .

V. THE AVALANCHE

Just then a crashing sound was heard,
That caused each ruddy cheek to blanch,
Though no one moved nor spoke a word,
All listening to the avalanche
With apprehensive ears intent,
Knew what a mountain snowslide meant.
Nor marvel that each visage paled,
Nor that the hardy sinews quailed;
These terrors of the solitude
The mountain's timbered slopes denude,

Sweeping the frozen spruce and fir
As with a snowy scimitar;
Nor can the stately pines prevent
Its irresistible descent;
A foe admitting no defence.
A moment passed in dire suspense,
And at its expiration brief,
Each heaved a breath of deep relief;
The snowslide, terrible and vast,
Had precipice and chasm leapt,
And down the rugged mountains swept,
Missing the cabin as it passed.

   .   .   .   .

The cabin clock had indicated five
When due composure was at length restored;
As evidence that all were still alive,
Queries were made about the "festive board,"
As sailors shipwrecked on some barren rock,
After the first excitement of the shock,
Mingle their words of gratitude and prayer
With speculations on the bill of fare.
No depth of danger man is called to face,
No exultation nor extreme disgrace,
No victory nor depression of defeat
Can shake recurrent Hunger from her seat.

The cabin oracle so often used,
A pack of playing cards, was soon produced.
A turn at whist the afternoon before,
Told who should cut the wood and sweep the floor.

As one of the disasters of defeat,
Washing the dishes fell to Russian Pete.
A game of freeze-out, played with equal zeal,
Decided who should cook the evening meal;
Conspiring cards electing Uncle Jim,
The culinary task devolved on him.

Accordingly, with acquiescent nod,
Abiding by the fortunes of the game,
This patriarch, so venerable and odd,—
Whose skill in cooking was of local fame,
Knocked out the ashes from his meerschaum pipe
And laid it tenderly upon the shelf,
Took a preliminary wash and wipe,
And squinting in the mirror at himself,
Like most of those possessed of little hair,
Brushed what he still had left with greatest care.
Small use for comb or brush had Uncle Jim,
His capillary wealth, a grayish rim
Or hirsute chaplet, as it had been called
By other miners less completely bald,
Fringing his head an inch above the ears,
Marked off his shining pate in hemispheres.
His flowing beard, of venerable air,
Enjoyed a strict monopoly in hair,
As if the raven curls that once adorned
His occiput, that habitation scorned
And took, as an expression of chagrin,
A change of venue to his ample chin.

When Uncle Jim was duly washed and groomed,
The running conversation was resumed,
And as the veteran his task pursued,
Mixing the biscuit dough with judgment good,
All smoked and talked, excepting Dad McGuire,
Who, helping Uncle Jim, stirred up the fire,
Raking the embers in a little pile,
Then warmed the old Dutch oven up a while,
And after greasing with a bacon rind,
The biscuit dough was to its depths consigned.

Soon from within the oven, partly hid
By embers piled upon the cumbrous lid,
The baking powder biscuits nestling there
With wholesome exhalations charged the air.
A pot of beans suspended by a wire
Swung like a pendulum above the fire,
And answered every flame's combustive kiss
With roundelay of bubble and of hiss,
While in the esculent commotion swam
The residue of what was once a ham.
Though epicures, who yearn for fowl and fish,
May scorn this plain and inexpensive dish,
So free from the extravagance of waste,
Yet succulent and pleasant to the taste,
Of all the varied products of the soil,
The bean is most esteemed by those who toil.
Removed, in place less prominent and hot,
One might have seen the old black coffee pot,

And watched the puffs of aromatic steam
Rise on the background of the firelight's gleam.
A pleasant sibilation filled the room,
As with an unctuous savor or perfume
The bacon sizzled in the frying-pan,
The bane and terror of dyspeptic man;
But those who labor for their daily bread
Of sedentary ills have little dread.

The simple yet salubrious repast
Was on the rustic table spread at last.
No cut-glass flashed and sparkled in the light,
Nor burnished silver service met the sight.
No butter dish, nor sugar bowl was seen,
The grains of sugar, white and saccharine,
Imprisoned in a baking powder can,
Rose in a wilderness of pot and pan.
The butter firkin stood upon a shelf
Where every one could reach and help himself.
The nibbling rodent and destructive moth
Found naught to lure them in the shape of cloth.
No tablespread of costly linen lent
Its white disguise or figured ornament
To catch the bacon or the coffee stain.
Nor was there cup or plate of porcelain,
For empty cans, stripped of their labels, bare,
And pie tins held the same positions there.

         .   .   .   .

All congregated 'round the simple spread
And ate the beans and baking powder bread,

With all the satisfaction and delight
That crown the hungry miner's appetite;
Not gluttony, that enemy to health,
That often follows in the trail of wealth,
But wholesome relish, which the laboring poor
Enjoy, who eat their fill, but eat no more.

The final course was ushered in at last,
When apple sauce around the board was passed;
As Uncle Jim stretched forth his hand across
The table to the dish of apple-sauce,
And on his ample pie tin placed some more,
A hurried knock resounded from the door,
And Steve McCoy, a miner in the camp,
With brow from snow and perspiration damp,
Rushed in, from out the white and whirling waste,
In the excitement incident to haste,
And waiving further ceremony cried:—
"Our cabin has been taken by a slide!"

Steve as a snowy Santa Claus appeared,
Pulling the icicles from off his beard,
Relating, in his intervals of breath,
His tale of dire disaster and of death;
He, and his partner "Smithy," were on shift
Within the tunnel working in a drift,
Chasing a stringer in their search for ore,
Within the hill a thousand feet or more.
The rock was hard and both of them were tired,
The holes were blasted as the work required;

Then to their consternation and surprise,
Upon emerging from the tunnel's mouth,
No hospitable cabin met their eyes
Upon the hillside, sloping toward the south;
The hut of logs where they had cooked and slept
Had been from human eyes forever swept.
Their partners, it were reason to presume,
Were suffocating in a snowy tomb.

"Smithy" had gone to Uncle Bobby Green,
Whose cabin lay the nearest to the scene,
To summon help, and get the boys to go
To probe with poles and shovels in the snow,
To find the living, or if life had sped,
To make the avalanche yield up its dead.
Of partners, Steve and Smithy had but two,
"Daddy" McLaughlin and young Dick McGrew,
Uncle and nephew, patriarch and youth,
Both men of strict integrity and truth.
Four other miners on another lease
Dwelt with the boys in harmony and peace.
Two strangers, who arrived the night before,
Had been invited, till the storm was o'er,
To share their hospitality.   Their fate
Had raised the list of dead, perhaps, to eight.

Ere Steve had panted forth his final word,
The boys had risen up with one accord;
The rescue must be tried at any cost,
The chance, however slight, must not be lost.

Steve as a runner who has reached his goal,
Leaned half exhausted on his snowshoe pole,
The while his sturdy auditors began
To don their caps and mittens, to a man,
Then wrapping mufflers 'round their ears and throats,
Put on their clumsy, canvas overcoats.
Thanks to the providence of Dad McGuire,
Who always kept a stock of baling wire
And odds and ends of everything around,
Their feet were quickly and securely bound
With canvas ore sacks or with gunny-sacks,
A thing the miner's wardrobe seldom lacks.

VI. THE RESCUE

Forth to the rescue went the miners bold,
Regardless of the tempest wild and brisk,
Regardless of the driving snow and cold,
Regardless of the hazard and the risk;
Facing with stalwart resolution brave
The snowy fate of those they strove to save.

One form of courage nerves the soldier's arm,
Excitement overcomes the wild alarm
Which at the onset e'en the bravest feel,
Though self-possession may that fear conceal.
The unromantic dangers of the storm
Require another and a sterner form,
For no emotion nerves the craven breast
To tempt the snowslide on the mountain's crest;

That noblest element unnoticed thrives
Beneath the surface in unnumbered lives;
At danger's call the sympathetic bond
Leaps to the surface, as the waves respond
When one has tossed a pebble in a pond;
For man has ever since the world began
Laid down his life to save his fellow-man;
Heroes are they, no praise commensurate,
Who do their duty in the face of fate.

Through gloomy forests, intricate and dark,
Which skirt the confines of the mountain park,
With arduous climb and hazardous ascent
Up through the gulch precipitous and wild
To where the avalanche its force had spent,
In silent haste the rescue party filed.

On such occasions little may be said,
The sternest use subdued and whispered breath,
For silence seems contagious from the dead,
A vague, unconscious reverence for death.
Facing the inconvenience of the blast,
Which whirled the drifting snowflakes as it passed,
The party shovelled; and with one accord
Abstained from converse, no one spoke a word
Till hours of strenuous search disclosed to sight
Six corpses from their sepulchre of white.
The other two, who by some wondrous means,
Escaped with but some trifling cuts and sprains,
Were in the meantime by their fellows found,

Dazed and exhausted in the gulch below,
For storm-bewildered men will grope around
Describing circles in the blinding snow,
Until they sink, their vital forces spent,
And crystal snowflakes weave their cerement.

Six pairs of skies,* each improvised a sled,
On which were placed the stark and staring dead;
As flickering lanterns flashed a ghostly glow
Upon them in their winding-sheets of snow,
The sad procession now retraced its course
Back through the dismal forest, while the blast
Wailed forth a requiem in accents hoarse,
Which shuddering pines re-echoed as it passed.

 . . . .

With sorely overtaxed and waning strength,
As some spent swimmer struggling to the shore,
The weary party found its way at length,
Back through the forest to the cabin's door.
As Uncle Jim, whose life was ever spent
In ministering to others, had been sent
Ahead, the dying coals had been renewed
With fresh supplies of pine and aspen wood,
And blazed a cheery invitation forth
To those who sought the comfort of the hearth.

The two survivors were the strangers who
Had just arrived the afternoon before;
Their names nor antecedents no one knew,
But western miners do not close the door

    * Norwegian snowshoes.

On weary travellers, whosoe'er they be,
No matter what their race or pedigree;
The one credential needed in the west
Is—human being, storm-bound and distressed.
The rescued miners, much benumbed and chilled,
To show some signs of conscious life began;
So Dad McGuire, in therapeutics skilled
To cure the maladies of beast or man,
Pursuant of his self-appointed task,
From out some secret depths produced a flask,
Which to the rescued miners he applied
As guaranteed to warm them up inside.
By way of chance digression, should you ask
The nature of the liquid in the flask,
Which, evidently, the boys had used before,
We must admit, the empty bottle bore,
Like most of bottles used in mining camps,
The revenue collector's excise stamps.

The senior of the rescued men appeared
In age to crowd the three-score years and ten;
Of stalwart form, with whitened hair and beard,
The peer of multitudes of younger men,
In matters appertaining to physique;
He first recovered and essayed to speak.
As Dad McGuire and kind old Uncle Jim
Were ministering as best they could to him,
In kindly interest they inquired his name,
"John T. McGuire," the labored answer came.

As Dad McGuire leaned over him to hear,
His gaze descried a mole behind his ear,
Then with an exclamation of surprise,
As one who scarcely can believe his eyes,
He turned the stranger over on his back,
Found two more moles,—and cried—"My brother
    Jack!"

   .   .   .   .
   .   .   .   .

Erratic as the vacillating wind,
Are the mysterious wanderings of the mind.
When reason lays her golden veil aside,
What vagaries and aberrations glide
Through the disordered precincts of the brain!
What phantoms rise and disappear again!
What curious blendings of reality
And fact, with wildest flights of phantasy!
The flickerings of reason's feeble light
And relaxation into mental night,
Seem as a beacon on some rock-bound coast,
Which flutters, wanes and disappears almost,
Then with a flash illuminates the shore,
Gleams for a moment and is seen no more;
Or on some starless midnight, when the storm
Dissolves in chaos each familiar form,
And robes the landscape in cimmerian pall,
The lightnings play,—then darkness covers all.

Unlocked by fever and delirium,
The cautious tongue becomes no longer dumb,

And with the nervous tension overwrought,
Oft gives expression to the secret thought.
'Twas thus the junior of the rescued men,
A modern Hercules, both fair and young,
With accent truly cosmopolitan,
Raved both in English and some unknown tongue.
His accents wild and unintelligible,
Devoid of meaning, on his hearers fell,
With the exception of the practised ear
Of Russian Pete, who stood beside him there,
And seemed from his expression to detect
Some most familiar tongue or dialect.

When reason, with a penetrating gleam,
Burst through the canopy of mental gloom,
As one awakening from a hideous dream,
He started up and stared about the room,
Until he chanced to catch the kindly eyes
Of Russian Pete, which kindled with surprise.
A look of mutual recognition passed
Between the men, so strangely joined at last.
All that the congregated miners heard
Was one, presumably a Russian word,
And Russian Pete, with joy-illumined face,
Held his lost brother in his kind embrace.

.   .   .   .
.   .   .   .

Dazed by exhaustion, comatose and deep,
The two survivors, while the tempest roared,

Were through the gentle ministry of sleep
To normal strength unconsciously restored.

'Tis human nature to review again
The stirring incidents of joy or pain;
So on the eve of the succeeding day,
When four-and-twenty hours had passed away,
The party grouped around the blazing light
Which from the fireplace streamed into the night,
And in its glow, so comfortable and warm,
Recounted the disasters of the storm.
Like some informal gathering, at first
All spoke at once, as with a common burst;
Then as the intermittent tempest wailed,
The talk subsided and a calm prevailed.
All watched the pitch ooze from the knots and burn,
Or smoked their pipes in silent unconcern.

Some moments passed, when Uncle Jim arose,
Nudged Dad McGuire, who seemed inclined to
     doze,
And as he started up and rubbed his eyes
Addressed him and the Russian in this wise:
"Two days ago the three of us confessed
The reasons, that impelled us to come West;
Now if it please your brethren to relate
The strange caprice of fortune or of fate,
Which led them hither,—after all these years,
The boys will listen with attentive ears."

VII. THE BLIGHT OF WAR

All eyes now sought the brother of McGuire,
Who sat apart, some distance from the fire
Smoking in silence, while the flickering light
Mingled its crimson with his locks of white;
He, with his flowing, patriarchal beard,
A sage, from some forgotten age, appeared,
Or wrinkled seer from some enchanted clime,
Whose eye could pierce the veil of future time.
There in the ever thickening haze of smoke,
He, being three times importuned,—awoke.

As from his corncob pipe and nostrils broke
The spiral wreaths of blue tobacco smoke,
Which formed a smoky halo, as they spread
A foot above his venerable head,
Resembling halos which the artist paints
O'er angel heads, or mediæval saints,
This man of years, so calm and circumspect,
Stroked his long beard, yawned twice and stood
　　erect.

Like to a wizard, or magician old,
With some mysterious secret to unfold,
This man, whose bearing would command respect,
Stepped forth and eyed his listeners direct;
Then waiving preludes or apologies,
Addressed his auditors in terms like these:

"These lips, which now their secret shall reveal,
For more than forty years have worn a seal.
For years as hunter, pioneer and scout,
I roamed the western solitudes about,
Not caring whether fortune smiled or not,
If memory's painful twinges were forgot.
I sought, as many other men have done,
Within the wilderness,—oblivion.
Work is the only sure iconoclast
For the unpleasant memories of the past;
So as a placer miner, prospector,
And half a dozen avocations more,
Within the city, and the solitude,
The star-eyed Goddess of Success I wooed.
Twice was I numbered with the men of wealth,
Twice lost I all, including strength and health.
For wealth, when fortune's fickle wheel revolves
Adversely, into empty air dissolves.
Till fate so strangely led my footsteps here,
Mine was, indeed, a versatile career.
Yet none my antecedents ever guessed,
Nor learned from me the cause that led me west.

This hair and beard which envy not to-night
The drifting snowbanks their unbroken white,
Methinks, as memory scans the backward track,
Vied with the raven's glossy coat of black,
When I, with some adventurous emigrants,
First crossed the plain's monotonous expanse,

To leave my former history behind.
But who can regulate his peace of mind,
Or drop the morbid burdens of the breast
By simply going east or coming west?

'Way down upon the Rappahannock's shore,
Enshrined in memory, though seen no more,
There lies an old plantation. There I drew
My infant breath, and into manhood grew.
Its fields are overgrown with willows now,
For more than forty years unturned by plough,
While war's red desolation razed to earth
The old stone manor-house that claimed my birth.

Ah, yes! 'Tis forty years ago, or more,
Since, standing near the old paternal door,
One pleasant morning in the early spring,
With some few friends and kinfolks visiting,
Two mounted neighbors stopped in passing by,
And reining up their horses hurriedly
Told us the news, which like a cannon ball
Sped through the land, announcing Sumter's fall.
The animus with which their comments fell,
I heard months later in the rebel yell.

In civil war or fratricide is found
No place for such as seek a middle ground.
Though lines of demarcation intervene,
No peaceful neutral zone may lie between.
'Tis not an easy thing to breast the tide
Of public sentiment, and to decide

In opposition, though the cause be right,
When crossing public sentiment means fight.
'Tis easier to let the moving throng
Without resistance carry you along.
When he who hesitates, or turns around,
May in the grist of public wrath be ground.
But men there are you cannot drive in flocks;
They dash like breakers, or resist like rocks.

Within my breast I fought my sternest fight,
I could not view the southern cause as right,
And yet I loved the people of the south;
Debating thus I opened not my mouth.
Both in my waking hours and in my dreams,
I heard the arguments of two extremes.
My conscience said: 'A uniform of blue
Awaits your coming, wear it and be true.'
My interests argued: 'Though the cause be wrong,
Your people have espoused it right along.
Your worthy family has for many years
Seen sorrow only in the white man's tears.
Desertion means to wear the traitor's brands,
And face your friends with muskets in their hands,
To slay them with the bayonet and ball,
Or by, perhaps, your brother's hand to fall.'

I heard the clarion accents of the fife
Fan into flames the dormant coals of strife.
With blast prophetic and reverberant swell,
I heard the bugle's echoing voice foretell

The coming conflict, while the brazen notes
Were answered by the cheers from many throats.
I heard the measured rattle of the drum,
Proclaiming that the day of wrath had come.
I heard harangues, incendiary and loud,
Meet with the approbation of the crowd.
I saw the faltering and irresolute,
Greeted with jeer and deprecating hoot.
I saw the threatening clouds of war increase,
Yet prayed for peace, where there could be no peace.
The winds of slavery their seed had sown;
That seed to rank maturity had grown;
The cup was full, and now from branch and root,
The whirlwind came to strip its lawful fruit.

I saw my friends and neighbors march away
With martial tread, in uniforms of gray.
I saw them raise their caps in passing by
And fair hands wave their kerchiefs in reply.
Then I, who had in military schools
Received some insight into army rules,
And, being of a martial turn of mind,
Was offered a commission, and,—declined.
My declination was a shock to all,
'Coward!' said they, 'to shun your country's call,—
Then stay at home, from wounds and scars exempt,
But pay the price,—your former friends' contempt.'

That action was, for me, the Rubicon,
Which crossed, I had no choice but follow on.

But what a change! The penalty was high,
My childhood's friends now passed me coldly by.
I, who had been a social favorite,
Received no salutation when we met.
Fair ones, who used to smile, now looked askance,
Or eyed me with a cold indifference.
My action seemed base cowardice in their eyes,
They knowing not my secret sympathies.
Though of a family rich and widely known,
I stood in the community, alone,
Like a pariah none would recognize,
Inaction was enough to ostracize.
I seemed to see, like Hagar's fated son,
Against me raised the hand of every one.

The time had come when I must make my choice,
Defend one side with musket and with voice;
Then I, to conscience and convictions true,
Seemed an apostate,—for I chose the blue.

There are inscriptions on the scrolls of fate
Which seem too bitter even to relate.
I waive the details,—better to conceal
The secret skeletons, than to reveal.
I shall not tell you how my brother stormed,
When he of my intentions was informed.
I pass the story, how my ringing ears
Were filled with threats, entreaties and with sneers.
And how with tear-stained face the maiden came,
Who was to be my bride and bear my name;

How she appealed to sentiment and pride,
Plead, supplicated,—then forsook my side;
And how one evening, in an angry burst,
My sire pronounced his favorite son accurst;
And how a mother, clinging to her child,
Saw son and father still unreconciled;
And how that father, pointing to the door,
Forbade that son to cross the threshold more;
'Go, go!' said he, 'but never more return!
Go, slay your neighbors, pillage, sack and burn!
But never while the golden sun doth shine,
Be welcomed home as son and heir of mine.'
I state not what in anger I replied,
For anger in my breast has long since died.
Renounced, despised and disinherited,
I trod the path of duty where it led,
And ten days later, in the rain and damp,
Stood as a sentry near a Union camp.

.   .   .   .

Fain from my recollections would I blot
These images, which time erases not,
And leave to history's undying page,
The recitation of those acts of rage.
Incarnadined with human blood appears
The record of the four succeeding years.
Black with the ruins of the vandal flame,
A carnival of misery and shame.
I must abridge, and if my hearers please,
Confine myself to generalities.

From first Manassas to the Wilderness,
A period of some four years,—more or less,
But anyway, till long in sixty-four,
A musket or a shoulder-strap I bore.
Though years have passed, I have remembrance yet
Of musketry and glistening bayonet.
As retrospective moods attune the ear
To memory's voice, again I seem to hear
The cannon's deep and minatory roar,
Like breakers dashing on a rock-bound shore.
The bursting bomb and fulminating shell,
Again their stories of destruction tell.

Again to-night, with memory's eye I view
The sanguinary scenes of sixty-two,
The march of infantry, the reckless dash
Of cavalry, with onslaught fierce and rash;
I see their sabres, glittering and bare,
Flash from their scabbards in the smoky air;
I hear the clatter of the horses' hoofs,
And see the smoke expand in greyish puffs;
As rifles flash and speed the deadly ball,
I see the riders from their horses fall;
Yet forward moves the furious attack,
The opposing column wavers and falls back;
I see the impact, combat hand to hand,
Horses and riders writhing on the sand;
I see the steeds with perspiration wet,
Sink on the well-directed bayonet;

I see them, wounded by the fatal lunge,
Become unmanageable and madly plunge;
Foaming and snorting with the sudden pain,
They trample on the wounded and the slain;
I see their riders in the stirrups stand
And grasp their pistols with the bridle hand;
I see the pistols flash and sabres thrust,
A scene of wild confusion, smoke and dust;
I hear the bugle sounding a retreat,
They now retire, their victory complete;
But mark the price paid for their brief success;
Horses with blood-stained saddles,—riderless.

I see an army bivouac on the field,
To nature's obdurate demands they yield,
And on the ground, from sheer exhaustion spent,
They lie without protecting roof or tent.
So silently their prostrate forms are spread,
One may not tell the sleeping from the dead.
I see, before the campfire's fitful gleam,
The sentry pace, as in a waking dream,
Yet manfully subduing the fatigue
Of battle, and the march of many a league,
For no excitement or emotion serves
To buoy his spirits or sustain his nerves.
Weak from the loss of their accustomed rest,
With heavy eyes and aching bones distressed,
The while their weary comrades soundly sleep,
The sentinels their lonely vigils keep,

As from the glittering expanse of skies,
The stars look down with cold, impassive eyes.

I see brigades, magnificent and large,
With bristling bayonets prepare to charge;
I see their banners in the distance gleam,
Reflecting back the sun's resplendent beam;
Within the shelter of the rifle pits,
Another army with composure sits,
While ever and anon a rifle's crack
Seems to invite the spirited attack.
From a commanding, wooded eminence,
By nature calculated for defence,
Upon the advancing regiments I see
The murderous belching of artillery;
I see their proud and militant array,
Before the deadly grapeshot melt away;
Before the rifle's supplementing breath,
Whole columns sink in ghastly heaps of death;
I see them close their gaps and press ahead,
But only to augment the list of dead;
I see them, stretched upon the burning sands,
Clutching the air with lacerated hands;
From underneath the mutilated heap,
The wounded, with great difficulty, creep;
Dragging a helpless arm, or shattered limb,
With reeling brain and sight confused and dim,
They grope, they crawl, or limp with painful tread;
Their uniforms no longer blue, but red;

And pinioned underneath the ghastly pile,
I hear them struggle for release the while;
But fainter, ever fainter grow their cries,
Fainter, and fainter still, their groans arise;
Weaker and weaker are their throes, until
With one last quivering throb, they too, are still.

I see the vultures, as they scent afar
Their portion in the reeking spoils of war;
Far in the distance scattering specks appear,
Which multiply in size as they draw near,
Until they balance with their pinions spread,
Or circle 'round the dying and the dead.

This is the realistic side of war,
Which most men overlook and all abhor,
Which differs from the sentiments conveyed
By spotless uniforms on dress parade.

.   .   .   .

War is a crucible that tries men's souls,
A drama, stern in all its various rôles;
Though saturated with all forms of crime,
'Tis celebrated in heroic rhyme;
Though opposite to every humane thought,
With murder, pillage and destruction fraught,
In literature, in history and art,
It forms the theme, or plays a leading part;
Though at the best, deplorable and bad,
'Tis yet with sentiment and romance clad;
Thus are the gory deeds of sword and fire,
Commemorated by the bardic lyre.

Its eras, though with tragedy replete,
Form stepping-stones whereon ambitious feet
May mount to prominence, perhaps to fame,
And write in crimson an illustrious name.
'Tis said that heroes are the fruits of war,
No matter what the struggle may be for,
As men will fight to make, or unmake laws,
Will fight for, or against the worthiest cause.
They must have heroes, though to make them drains
The life-blood from the nation's noblest veins.
And though no vocal adulations rise,
Their heroes many men apotheosize.
Man is so strangely constituted, he
Must hero-worshipper, or hero be,—
So give him heroes, let the armies bleed,
And he will worship them with word and deed;
Though down within their breasts most men prefer
To be the hero, than the worshipper.

To gain the plaudits of the multitude,
The warrior, with ambitious zeal imbued,
Climbs upward, and accomplishing his ends
To take his share of worship condescends,
Forgetting that his honors are bedewed
With human tears and based on human blood.

Some streaks, in military pomp, we see,
That savor much of pride and vanity,
As thirst for notoriety and fame
Has often fanned the patriotic flame.

Though one might think that men would be content
To pluck one star from glory's firmament,
Yet, when they mount the ladder a few rounds,
Their envy and ambition know no bounds.
To wear the epaulette and strut with pride,
Makes men forget that war is homicide.

Some call it fate, some call it destiny,
Some call it accident; what'er it be,
It seems that some have been created for
The honors, some, the sacrifice of war.

.   .   .   .

When I enlisted as a raw recruit,
Promotion was no object of pursuit,
But liking honor more than sacrifice,
On shoulder-straps I soon cast envious eyes.
For one rash act,—'twas counted bravery,
Good fortune made a corporal of me.
Soon, as if favored by some lucky charm,
I wore a sergeant's stripes upon my arm.
Twice was I wounded, twice resumed the field
Before my wounds had been completely healed.
I carry yet, and shall until I die,
A musket ball, encysted in my thigh.
Twice was I captured, twice as prisoner
Drank I the dregs from out the cup of war.
As if some guardian star my course arranged,
Once I escaped, and once was I exchanged.
Then, as lieutenant, rose I from the ranks,
Received a medal and a vote of thanks.

The ladder of promotion, round by round,
I soon ascended and henceforth was found
Among the few selected favorites
Whom fortune decks with stars and epaulettes.
Though liking not the rôle of matador,
Within the ruthless theatre of war,
From private soldier every part I played,
Until my sword directed a brigade.
I wore, the night before I started west,
Four medal decorations on my breast.

The war progressed, for time rolls on the same
In peace or war, and sixty-three became
A chapter in the annals of the past.
When sixty-four was ushered in at last,
To write in characters of blood and fire
Its page of human immolation, dire,
The waiting army lay encamped, before
The Rapidan's inhospitable shore.
The first few weeks, devoid of incident,
Were in the army's winter quarters spent,
Until the winter, on his snowy wing,
Retired before the genial breath of spring.
In speculation on the moves to come,
The tongue of prophecy remained not dumb,
But showered prognostications of defeat,
Succeeded by the usual retreat,
When rumors of offensive action planned
As spring approached, were spread through each
    command.

Until the troops were mobilized and massed,
Until the final orders had been passed,
The veterans, who had remembrance still,
Recounted Fredericksburg and Chancellorsville.

But soon the dreadful Wilderness campaign,
With its long lists of wounded and of slain,
Vied with the carnage of the year before,
If it be possible to measure gore.
The tactics had been changed, for no retreat
Was ordered, as the sequel of defeat;
Instead of faltering or turning back,
There came another furious attack,
Another movement with invasive tread,
And, Spottsylvania claimed its heaps of dead.
Defeated, but uncrushed and undismayed,
The weakened corps, including my brigade,
With sadly thinned and decimated ranks,
Was hurled once more against the rebel flanks.
There in a hurricane of shot and shell,
One-half of its surviving numbers fell;
'Twas thus Cold Harbor's quarry made complete
The trio of victorious defeat.

Three Southern victories, yet like a knell
Upon the Southern ear these triumphs fell;
For those who perished in that dismal waste,
Had fallen and could never be replaced.
Though stubbornly contested inch by inch,
The lines were tightened like a horse's cinch.

We watched the Southern forces day by day,
From natural abrasion, wear away.

.   .   .   .

One evening as the disappearing light,
Unveiled the beauties of a cloudless night,
With much diminished numbers, my brigade
Its camp beside the Rappahannock made,
Some five miles distant from the spot of earth
Associated with my humble birth.

Next morning, ere the twinkling stars had set,
While officers and men were sleeping yet,
A courier rode up to my command,
And placed a cipher message in my hand;
Then spurring well his horse of dapple grey,
With parting salutation rode away.
This was the import of that message stern:
'Lay waste the district. All the fences burn.
Leave not a house or stable unconsumed.'
My father's house among the rest was—doomed.
I read that message and my anger blazed,
My home to be, by my own orders, razed!

A vision rose before my swimming brain,
I saw the old parental roof again,
I saw my father, as in days of yore,
Smoking his pipe beside the open door;
I saw his gaze, with penetrating look,
Fixed on the pages of some wholesome book;

I saw my mother sit beside him, there,
Recumbent in her old reclining chair.
The vision changed,—I saw her parting tears,
My father's parting curse rang in my ears;
'Go! Go!' said he, 'but nevermore return,
Go, slay your neighbors, pillage, sack and burn,
But never while the golden sun doth shine
Be welcomed home as son and heir of mine.'

I felt but little longing to return,
And less desire to pillage, sack and burn.
And yet,—those cruel orders I must give,
No power had I to voice the negative.
In commonplace affairs of life, 'tis true,
Men may elect to do, or not to do.
In military operations, they
Have no alternative, but to obey.

Ah! Fain, from that impending holocaust
Would I have snatched them! Rather had I lost
The tinselled honors and the epaulettes,
And doffed my uniform without regrets,
Than harm by word or deed that agèd sire;
Yet I must start, who fain would quench the fire.
I read and read that cipher message there,
How many times, I have not to declare,
But over and again I scanned the lines,
And pondered well its symbols and its signs;
Ironclad were they, from every standpoint viewed,
Admitting not of choice or latitude;

So, to the officers of my command,
I gave their orders, with a trembling hand,
And swift as horseflesh ever travelled, went
To seek the corps commander in his tent,
To crave this boon, or favor, at his hand,—
My father's house be still allowed to stand.

'Twas long before I gained an audience;
I felt, but cannot picture the suspense
Of that long hour's involuntary wait;
Too late, my heart would beat, too late, too late!
I took a seat and pulled my watch out once;
'Too late, too late,' the timepiece ticked response!
I paced the ground with quick, impatient tread;
'Too late, too late, too late,' my footsteps said!
'Too late, too late, too late!' With fluttering beat
My heart responded to my echoing feet.

The General, who a kindly heart possessed,
No sooner heard, than granted my request;
'Twas but a moment's work to mount my steed,
And spur him to his maximum of speed;
The faithful creature seemed to understand
And needed little urging from my hand,
As down the turnpike, toward my childhood's home,
He fairly flew, his bridle white with foam;
His hoofbeats, as we clattered o'er the ground,
Returned a dull, premonitory sound,
Which seemed to echo and accentuate
The burden of my heart, 'Too late! Too late!'

The fences, near the turnpike, as we passed,
Were by my orders disappearing fast;
The rails were piled in heaps and soon became
A prey to war's red ally,—vandal flame.
Houses, familiar to my childish sight,
Glowed strangely with an unaccustomed light,
While from adjacent barns and hay-ricks broke
Incipient tongues of flame and clouds of smoke.
The orders, ruthless and inflexible,
Were by the soldiers executed well.

Still down the turnpike dashed my sweating horse,
I plied the cruel spurs with double force,
When in the distance there appeared to view
The old stone manor-house my childhood knew.
My spirit sank,—though I was not surprised,
My worst misgivings had been realized,
For from the roof and upper windows came
Dense clouds of smoke and lurid sheets of flame.
It had its portion in the common fate,
'Too late!' the mocking hoof-beats rang, 'Too late!'

We passed a company, on their return
From executing those instructions stern;
It was the company of my brigade
Wherein I first was a lieutenant made;
Its officers and men I knew by name;
They cheered me when their captain I became;
They cheered me when I left a major's tent,
To be the colonel of their regiment.

They did my bidding. How could I condemn!
They honored me and I respected them;
And yet, these favorites of my command
Had not one hour before applied the brand
Which was transforming with its wand of fire
My father's house into—his funeral pyre.

That they had met resistance, I could see,
For wounded men, in number two or three,
Were by their comrades carted in advance,
While one more limped behind the ambulance.
Upon a stretcher carried in their van,
The soldiers bore the body of a man;
He was their captain, and my bosom friend;
He plied that torch,—and met a bloody end.

I plunged the spurs, but not without remorse,
Into his steaming flanks and urged my horse,
Which I disliked to tax beyond his strength;
Such speed had he maintained, that now, at length,
He was compelled to pant and hesitate;
With labored effort we dashed through the gate,
Or where the gate had been an hour before,
For gate and fence alike, were seen no more,
Save in the scattered bonfires, while at most
All that remained was here and there a post.

There was a fascination in that sight
Which seemed to conquer and unnerve me, quite;
A sense of horror, not akin to fear,
Possessed my being as we galloped near;

All sorts of evil pictures filled my mind,
As one who seeks, yet dreads what he may find;
As we drew nearer, I remember well,
With hissing crash the roof collapsed and fell;
Dismounting, I the premises surveyed,
And viewed the havoc and destruction made;
Crushed by the disappointment, the suspense,
And failure of my planned deliverance,
I moved about with apprehensive tread,
To seek my relatives, alive or dead;
And, near a haystack's smouldering ruins found
My father's body, weltering on the ground;
A musket tightly clenched within his hand,
Slain by the troopers of my own command;
His whitened locks were streaked with crimson
    stains,
The same red blood then coursing through my veins.

Close by his side, a form with silvered hair,
Caressed his brow, with dazed, abstracted air;
'Twas she who nursed my being into life,
The highest type of mother and of wife;
Our glances met, yet e'er I framed to speak,
She started up, then with a piercing shriek
Fell back, expiring on the speechless clay
Of him whose life so lately ebbed away.

.   .   .   .

As campfires gleamed, and heaven's orb, serene
With borrowed radiance, o'erflowed the scene,

Within a grave, beneath the crimson sands,
I laid them both to rest with my own hands.
In lieu of prayer, or solemn dirge, was heard
The twittering cadence of the mockingbird,
Uniting with the sentry's muffled tread,
Which seemed a measured requiem for the dead,
As, side by side, in death's eternal sleep,
I laid them tenderly, nor paused to weep,
For feelings which in tears find no relief
Had dried the very fountainheads of grief.
I shaped a double mound above their clay,
Planted a wooden cross,—and went my way.

   .   .   .   .

That night I tore the medals from my breast,
Resigned my sword and started for the West."

VIII. THE STORY OF AN EXILE

Such was the tragic story told,
And, tired from standing on his feet,
This patriarch so gray and old
Relit his pipe and took a seat.
As one, inert and overtaxed
From strenuous toil, he soon relaxed
Into that dull composure, which
Fatigue accords to poor and rich.

The observation could detect
No levity nor disrespect,

Nor through his story was there heard
Remark or interruptive word,
His voice and bearing as he spoke,
Admitting not of jest or joke.
The common feeling seemed to be
Respect and deepest sympathy.

As childish incidents recurred
In memory to Dad McGuire,
As one who neither saw nor heard
He sat, intent upon the fire;
Yet watched the ever-changing blaze
With that intensity of gaze
Which shows the things the eyes have caught
Are not the subjects of the thought,
But far beyond their metes and bounds
The vision rests on other grounds.

This story of a life rehearsed,
Left other eyes bedimmed and blurred;
Each with his silent thoughts conversed
And none presumed to speak a word,
Lest sympathy the tears provoke.
Old Uncle Jim forgot to smoke
And though he had replenished it,
Still left his meerschaum pipe unlit,
Till as the watchdog suddenly
Wakes up with apprehensive sniff,
He started from his reverie
And took an unsuccessful whiff;

But embers which the fire supplied
Soon changed the fragrant charge inside
With alternating draw and whiff,
Into a meerschaum Teneriffe.

All smoked, excepting Dad McGuire,
Who stirred the embers of the fire,
And placed thereon what seemed to be,
The remnants of a hemlock tree;
'Twas one of those ungainly stumps,
Composed of twisted knots and bumps,
Which every boy or even man,
In chopping wood, skips if he can;
'Twas such a chunk as may be seen
After the woodpile's chopped up clean;
The log they split the blocks upon
And leave when all the rest is gone.
This chunk, which none of them could split,
Though many had attempted it,
By divers and ingenious ways,
Was soon enveloped in a blaze,
Which shed its glare into the night,
As beacons radiate their light.

Reclining by his brother's side,
Abstracted and preoccupied,
The Russian, rubicund and hale,
Was importuned to tell his tale,
And slightly coughing from the smoke,
Forthwith in faultless diction spoke: -

"My brother's story you have heard,
The same should mine be, word for word,
Up to that dismal dungeon grate,
Which he presumed had sealed my fate.
I doubt not he related well
The horrors of that loathsome cell,
So that description, now by me,
Would fruitless repetition be.
Sufficient be it to declare
That brief was my detention there.

Though discontent the action was
Which constituted my offence,
I felt the weight of Russian laws
When chained to other malcontents.
Before the chains had time to rust
I plodded through the mud and dust
As many exiles erst had trod,
Their footprints often stained with blood.
With clanking chains and painful stride,
With Cossack guards on either side,
We marched in silence, in the reach
Of sabres that discouraged speech.
A sad procession, for full well
Our destinations could we tell.
Down country lane and village street
We limped with bruised and blistered feet,
In single file, as some infirm
Though monstrous centipede or worm,

Beset by some tormenting foe,
Might move with locomotion slow,
And tortured by its enemy,
Propel its foul dimensions by.

Past where the Urals, bleak and high,
Invade the cerulean sky
With summits desolate and gray,
With weary tread we wound our way.
Where intertwining branches made
A vernal canopy of shade,
The song-birds, from their arches high
Mocked at our chains, as we passed by;
The only forms of earth or air,
Deprived of rightful freedom there.

At night in forest depths profound,
We lay upon the cheerless ground,
Where on our route we chanced to be,
Nor couch nor coverlet had we
Between us and the turf or stones,
To soothe our tired and aching bones.
Our limbs emaciated grew,
Ragged were we and dirty, too,
As o'er the trans-Slavonian plains,
We dragged our grievous weight of chains.

As passed the autumn months away
Six leagues we measured every day,

Six leagues our loads were daily borne,
On shoulders galled and callous-worn.
Each morning was our march begun,
Before the advent of the sun,
While every evening in the west
He sank, before we paused for rest.
Time and again upon the road,
The weaker dropped beneath their load,
And fainting from fatigue and pain,
They sank, but rose not up again.

Where the Pacific's broad expanse
Of sleeping waters, calm and fair,
Divide the mighty continents
With their pelagic barrier;
Upon the Asiatic shore,
Some twelve leagues from the sea or more,
In course of time, our weary line
Was halted at a penal mine.
'Twas there within a log stockade
Constructed in a manner crude,
That we our habitation made
Through many months of servitude.

A mine's a mine the world around,
A cheerless place wherever found,
Dismal and dark beyond compare
And charged with foul, unwholesome air,
Which fills the lungs at every breath
With germs of an untimely death.

In caverns subterranean,
With limbs not bound by gyve or chain,
Of those who toil, few are the men
Who reach the threescore years and ten.
Such was the smoke-polluted mine
Wherein we slaved from morn till night,
Or when the sun had ceased to shine
We toiled till his returning light,
Then dragged each one his ball and chain
Back to his bed of straw again.
Day after day could there be seen
The same monotonous routine;
Such was the drudging life we led
Till hope from every bosom fled,
And each became as time rolled on
A spiritless automaton.

The details of a captive's lot
I fear would interest you not,
So your forbearance I beseech,
While, in impromptu forms of speech,
I strive in simple terms to shape
The narrative of my escape.

. . . .

From out the realms of tropic heat,
Invading with contagious feet,
Came there a plague, one summer-tide.
Up from the south with fatal stride
It stalked, and poured its vials forth
Upon the sparsely settled North;

A wave of pestilence and fear
Swept o'er the northland far and near;
The frenzied peasants, in their fright,
Sought safety in promiscuous flight;
In consternation and alarm,
To seek immunity from harm,
They left the sick in their distress,
And fled into the wilderness;
As if, within the solitude,
The Nemesis, which had pursued,
Might satiate its deadly wrath,
And deviate or change its path,
And its malignant steps retrace
Back to the southern starting-place.

The able-bodied left behind
The paralyzed, the halt and blind;
The well in abject terror fled,
Forsook the dying, while the dead,
Unburied in the summer breeze,
Became a nidus of disease,
Wherefrom fresh seeds of pestilence
Were scattered by the elements.

Of those who felt its loathsome breath,
But few escaped a speedy death;
So rapid were the ravages
Of that distemper or disease,
That many, stricken in the night,
Expired before the dawn of light;

For some, who in the morning time
Stood well and strong in manhood's prime,
The noontide brought the fatal scourge,
And evening zephyrs played the dirge;
Those who survived the plague direct
Oft died from hunger and neglect;
The convalescents woke and found
No ministering forms around,
No watcher sitting by the bed,
Alone were they, save for the dead;
They called, but Echo's voice alone
Answered the supplicating moan;
They prayed, but no one heard their prayer,
Then perished from the want of care.

The suffering of the stricken then,
Defies descriptive word or pen;
I see with memory's vision yet
The beads of suppurating sweat
Stand on the burning brows of those
Smitten with agonizing throes;
As racking tortures permeate
Each swollen and distorted shape,
With thirst which none may mitigate,
They call for drink with mouths agape;
Yet naught may succor such distress,
Save coma and unconsciousness;
When these the intellect benumb,
The sense and feeling overcome,

Within its tuneful cavern hung
No longer rests the fluent tongue,
But swollen by the pain and drouth,
Protrudes from out the parching mouth;
The burning and discolored lip
Imagined moisture tries to sip;
Again they vainly strive to speak
Their fevered incoherencies,
But vocal organs parched and weak
Respond but labored gasp and wheeze.

I scent the putrefying air,
And see the horror and despair
Depicted on the lineaments
Of every stricken countenance;
I see them writhe, then suddenly,
With ghastly leer convulse and die.

As stagnant waters generate
A fungous and unsightly freight
Of morbid scum and slimy moss,
Of origin spontaneous;
So latent germs, unnoticed, lurk
In readiness for deadly work;
When these the right conditions find,
And spread infection to the wind,
Chronologers, both far and near,
Record an epidemic year.

Within the bounds of our stockade,
The plague its foul appearance made,

And soon inoculated there,
Its virus to the very air,
Till e'en the genial summer breeze
Seemed a dispenser of disease;
Then, as impartial lightnings strike
The nobleman and serf alike,
Within this filthy prison yard,
It smote both prisoner and guard;
The difference of race, of lot,
Of rank was speedily forgot,
As discipline succumbed to dread
And officers and soldiers fled,
Save such as, fallen by the way,
Helpless and unattended lay,
Till death brought silence and relief,
From agony intense, though brief.

Within the walls of the stockade
Not one unstricken person stayed,
Except some convicts who remained
For one good reason :—we were chained.
Our dingy quarters, floor and bed,
Were filled with dying and with dead;
The only shelter we could claim,
A fetid lazar-house became.
I need not tell you how the air
Was filled with accents of despair,
How clamor and entreaty smote
The air, from blistered tongue and throat,

As burning rash and ghastly rheum
Supplanted nature's ruddy bloom;
How moan and outcry, curse and prayer
Were mingled with each other there;
Some raved in dialects unknown,
Or terms provincial, while the groan,
The common tongue of suffering men,
Was echoed ever and again.

Some, with reluctant clutch and gasp,
Saw life receding from their grasp;
And some, with stoic countenance,
Maintained a stern indifference,
For what are death's abstruse alarms,
When life is shorn of all its charms;
As zealots, when they come to die,
Lift their enraptured gaze on high,
And clasp to the expiring breast
Some crucifix or icon blest,
And mutter with stertorious breath
Some sacred word or shibboleth,
Then sink expectant and resigned,
As if in death a boon to find,
Some in excruciating pain,
Welcomed its foul destroying breath
And sought from cruel gyve and chain
Emancipation, though in death.

'Tis not my purpose to declare
The horrors which befell us there,

As passed the fatal hours away,
Of that most memorable day.
Each hour increased our dire distress,
Yet found our numbers less and less,
Till when the shadows overspread,
The major number were the dead.
But three survived that awful night,
To gaze upon the morning light;
And when the noonday breezes blew,
That three had been reduced to two;
And ere the setting of the sun
I was the sole remaining one.
A silence strangely mute and dumb
Succeeded pandemonium.

There when my last companion died,
Chained to a corpse on either side,
Strange as may seem the miracle,
I never felt more strong and well,
Nor held my life in less esteem;
In that position most extreme,
By silent death surrounded, I
Enjoyed . weird immunity.

'Twould serve no purpose to recite
My feelings, as approaching night,
With his impenetrable pall,
Descended and enveloped all.
I sat alone in fear and dread,
Chained to the floor,—and to the dead.

A gruesome and revolting sight
Is horrifying in the light,
But when dissembling night conceals,
The breast a double terror feels.
That darkness, black beyond compare,
Seemed a fit mantle for despair.
Few are the words when hope has failed;
An awful quietude prevailed;
I sat, a mute and helpless lump,
And felt my heart's pulsating thump,
With movement regular and strong,
Propel life's crimson flood along,
But made no sound until the spell
Of silence was unbearable.

I spoke, but all the ears in reach
Were deaf to every charm of speech;
I shouted till the roof, the floor
And walls resounded with the roar;
I called the dead men at my side,
But Echo's voice alone replied;
I was alone, nor man nor bru e
Was there, save those so stark and mute;
My voice upon my listening ear
Fell, most unnatural and queer,
As if with weird, uncanny sound
The walls responsive voices found,
And echoed back the tones at will,
To mock those tongues so cold and still;

Though these vociferations made
My spirit none the less afraid,
The silence seemed more terrible;
Words fail me as I strive to tell
How in my desperation, I
Abandoned hope, yet could not die.

I never craved the morning light,
As through that terrifying night,
For gentle but erratic Sleep
Withheld her respite soft and deep,
As in that charnel house I lay,
Till twilight ushered in the day.

When daylight had returned again
I strove with the relentless chain,
Twisted and tugged until at length
A more than ordinary strength
Possessed my arm, and at one stroke
The rivets weakened, bent and broke;
One master wrench and from the floor,
The ring which held the chain I tore;
I dragged the dead men o'er the ground
Till forge and anvil I had found;
There with the hammer, rasp and file
I wrought with diligence the while;
At some expense of time and pains,
I disengaged the cruel chains,
And stood once more erect and free;
Thus ended my captivity.

    .   .   .   .

A guard lay prostrate on the sand,
His rifle in his lifeless hand;
I wrenched it from his rigid clutch,
Then played the ghoul in self-defence,
For clothing and accoutrements
Escaped not my despoiling touch;
I breathed the air of liberty,
Alone I stood, but armed and free.
To mislead any watchful eyes,
I donned a militant disguise,
And, in the dead man's uniform,
Was soon prepared for strife or storm.

Unseen, unhindered, unpursued,
I soon was in the solitude,
Contending with impediments,
Which every wilderness presents.
Primeval forests, through which poured
Rivers unknown to bridge or ford;
Swamps, overgrown with weeds and moss,
Almost impossible to cross;
A waste of fallen trees and logs,
Rank vegetation, stagnant bogs;
Decaying leaves, profusely spread,
Which rustled at the slightest tread,
While underbrush and thicket made
A thorny maze or barricade,
Through which 'twas difficult to force
A passage or retain one's course.

There my experience began,
Along the lines of primal man;
My fare, as I remember well,
Was strictly aboriginal,
For stupid grouse and ptarmigan
Were easily approached and slain;
And, as a relish for such food,
I had the berries of the wood.

Through arches of umbrageous shade
I journeyed onward undismayed,
And undisturbed by man or beast,
Made daily progress toward the east,
Till viewing the Pacific shore,
Northward along the coast I bore.
I kept that course for many days,
Where none but savage eyes might gaze;
 Full many a mile my footsteps led
Through regions uninhabited,
Till where Kamschatka's barren rocks
Resist the sea's aggressive shocks,
One gloomy afternoon, I stood
And watched the wide and trackless flood.

'Twould make a tedious tale, I fear,
Not meet for recitation here,
Should I endeavor to relate
The details of a hermit's fate.
To all appearance I was free;
A plethora of liberty

Is little consolation, where
One lonely recluse breathes the air;
For solitary mortals find
But little joy and peace of mind;
When freedom is enjoyed alone,
Its fondest attributes are flown;
Men of companions destitute
Sink to the level of the brute;
Their sacred essence seems to be
Dependent on community.

Each morning, in the reddening skies,
Alone, I watched the sun god rise,
While every evening in the west,
Alone, I watched him sink to rest.
To catch a passing ship, in vain
I hourly scanned the watery plain,
Till one fair morn a distant sail
Brought the conclusion of my tale.

The whaler, such she proved to be,
Steered landward through a rippling sea,
And made directly for the shore;
She anchored, then I saw them lower
The ship's long-boat; at a command
I saw them row, then saw them land.
Fearing occasion might require
The service of a signal fire,
A mass of driftwood I had heaped;
Behind that pile I hid and peeped.

From that concealed position, I,
Watching with closest scrutiny,
Discovered that the squad of ten
Were not my fellow-countrymen.

Their purpose I could now discern;
One had a spade, which turn by turn
Each wielded till their willing hands
Had delved a grave within the sands.
Six of the party I espied
Returning to the long-boat's side,
Where from its bottom they began
To raise the body of a man,
In canvas strips securely sewed,
All ready for its last abode;
From every motion it would seem
The object of sincere esteem.
From my location I could see
Them balance it most tenderly,
As on six shoulders broad and strong,
They bore it sorrowfully along,
While wind and ever-restless surge
Joined in a requiem or dirge.

The sun through hazy Autumn skies
Shone on the simple obsequies,
As round the open grave they stood,
In reverential attitude,
And shovelled in the brown sea sand;
One, with a prayer-book in his hand,

Essayed the rôle of corybant;
Omitting the accustomed chant,
He read a burial service there,
Concluding with its words of prayer:
'Ashes to ashes! Dust to dust!'
These words of that abiding trust,
In life beyond the fleeting span
Which heaven has accorded man;
Elysian fields, where perfect peace
Succeeds life's transitory lease;
The inextinguishable fire
Of faith, the daughter of desire,
Glows brightest, when the faltering breath
Is conscious of approaching death;
Bent 'neath the weight of many years,
The form of hoary age appears,
E'en as the failing hourglass shows
That life is drawing to its close,
And when the final sands are spent,
The trembling limbs make their descent
Into the shadows, while the ray
Of faith illuminates the way.
Vain introspection, which descries
No light behind the mysteries
Of death, engenders in the breast
But vacant yearnings and unrest;
Relying on the eye of hope,
We look beyond our mundane scope,
And with enraptured vision see
The fore-gleams of futurity.

With eager eyes I watched them stand,
Upon that barren waste of sand,
Until the final words of prayer
Had died away upon the air.
Their words, euphonious and clear,
Were wafted to my listening ear,
Borne on a favorable breeze
Which blew directly from the seas;
My breast, with deep emotion stirred,
I recognized their every word,
An English burial ritual read,
On this wild shore, above the dead.
This dissipated every fear,
I knew deliverance was near;
My secret would be safe among
The scions of the English tongue.

Forever from the light of day
They laid his pallid form away,
While every word and action proved
Their rites were over one they loved.
Soon from the level of the ground,
There rose another silent mound,
To teach, beside that northern sea,
Its lesson of mortality.

Death on that dismal northern main,
In binding with its silent chain
Forever their lamented mate,
Had freed me from a sterner fate.

Leaving my earstwhile hiding place,
I stood before them face to face;
Then in their own vernacular,
Gave proper salutation there.
'Twas plain that they regarded me
As human salvage, which the sea
Had, in some evil moment, tossed
Upon that bleak and barren coast,
Like broken wreckage or debris,
Cast up by the capricious sea.
With frank but sympathetic eyes,
They watched me with no small surprise,
While I rehearsed without delay,
My story as a castaway.

Repairing to the ship's long-boat,
Which soon was in the surf afloat,
I bade farewell to Russian soil
In language not intensely loyal.
They ministered to my distress,
From ample stores of food and dress,
Performed such acts of kindness then
As might beseem large-hearted men;
Nor was there aught perfunctory
In their solicitude for me;
Their acts were of their own accord,
Without suspicion of reward.

Although possessed of little skill
In nautical affairs, to fill

A seaman's watch I volunteered,
As we toward Arctic waters steered,
Pursuant of the spouting whale;
I plied each task with rope ahd sail,
And ere we reached a harbor bar,
Was rated as a first-class tar;
By sufferance of as brave a crew
As ever sailed a voyage through,
The two succeeding years I passed
In northern seas before the mast;
Two years from that eventful day
We moored in San Francisco Bay.
I bade the sea farewell for aye,
Bade my deliverers good-bye,
With fervent pressure of the hand,
Then straight betook myself to land.

．　　．　　．　　．　　．　　．　　．　　．

Seeking a home with freedom blest,
I've cast my fortunes with the West."

IX. CONCLUSION

Concluding, he resumed his seat
Beside his brother, Russian Pete;
Yet ever and anon expressed
His views on points of interest,
And details, which this narrative
In its abridgment may not give,
As Dad McGuire and Uncle Jim
By turns interrogated him.

To say his hearers listened well,
Were too self-evident to tell,
For some who dozed before he spake,
Woke up and then remained awake.

As all the inclination felt,
To play a game, the cards were dealt;
The winners, it was understood,
To be exempt from chopping wood;
While he who made the lowest score
Must build the fire and sweep the floor.
Time spread his wings, the moments flew
Unheeded for an hour or two,
Until at length the measured stroke
Of twelve, in timely accents broke
From an old clock upon the shelf,
As old as Uncle Jim himself;
A good old clock, as old clocks go,
But usually too fast or slow,
But near enough the proper time
To serve the purpose of this rhyme.

The honors passed to Russian Pete,
When Dad McGuire sustained defeat,
As mighty warriors often do,
In some Chalons, or Waterloo;
The fortunes of the final game,
Adding fresh laurels to his fame;
Then all abstained from further play,
And forthwith put the cards away.

  •   •   •   •   •   •   •   •

'Twas passing late, the dying fire
Served as the summons to retire,
And soon the gentle wand of sleep,
Which works the dream god's drowsy will,
Laden with slumbers soft and deep,
Passed over them and all was still.

. . . .
. . . .

The storm was over, far and near,
The heavens shone, so cold and clear
That nebulæ and satellites,
Unseen on ordinary nights,
Now filled the broad expanse of sky
With unaccustomed brilliancy;
The astral vacuums and voids,
Were filled with discs and asteroids;
Dissevering the firmament,
The Milky Way disclosed to sight
Its pearly avenue of white
With planetary crystals blent;
Transparently it shone, and pale,
As some celestial gauze or veil;
A silvery baldric o'er the gold
Of constellations manifold.

A silence, undisturbed, prevailed,
The wind no longer moaned and wailed,
The elements had worked their will
And now were motionless and still;

From forest growth or underbrush
No whisper broke the solemn hush;
The tempest king on airy waves,
Retreated to his secret caves,
And chained the winds, which his behest
Had lately stirred to wild unrest.

The clouds had vanished, not a trace
Remained upon the arch of space,
To interpose a curtain rude
Between earth and infinitude;
Pellucid as the vault o'erhead,
The snows a layer of beauty spread,
Save where the genii of the storm
Had fashioned in fantastic form,
With alternating whirl and sift,
The pendent comb and massive drift.

The wilderness of ice and snow,
Transfigured with a mellow glow,
Received from the translucent skies
The stellar groups and galaxies;
A record of the starry waste,
By Nature's faultless pencil traced;
The vernal phalanxes of pine,
In cassocks clear and crystalline,
Seemed as a mirror, in whose sheen
The glimmering lamps of night were seen.
The replica of pearl and gem,
In heaven's twinkling diadem;

Golconda's treasury displayed,
On background of the forest shade.

Divested of their transient green,
By Autumn winds in wanton rage,
The aspen's leafless limbs were seen
Festooned with frosty foliage;
As fell upon their vestal white,
The placid moon's aspiring light,
The noble spruce and stately fir,
Stood draped with feathery garniture;
Configurated and embossed,
With lace and tapestry of frost,
In quaint and curious design,
The willows and the underbrush,
Were crystallized in silvery plush,
And shimmered in the cold moonshine.

.   .   .   .

The azure dome of space o'erhead,
With scintillating grandeur spread,
Looked down with cold inquiring eyes,
On earth with all her mysteries;
The while reflecting in their snows,
These glittering jewels of the night,
The mountains lay in calm repose,
Slumbering 'neath their robes of white.

[THE END]

DOLORES

I will sing of a quaint old tradition,
　A legend romantic and strange,
Which was whispered to me by the pine trees
　High up on the wild mountain range.
Far away in the mystical Westland,
　From the mountain peaks crested with snow,
Glides Dolores, the river of sorrow,
　Dolores, the river of woe.

Time was when this river of sorrow
　Had never a thought to be sad,
But meandered in joy through the meadows,
　With bluebell and columbine clad.
Her ripples were ripples of laughter,
　And the soft, dulcet voice of her flow
Was suggestive of peace and affection,
　Not accents of anguish and woe.

Long ago, ere the foot of the white man
　Had left its first print on the sod,
A people, both free and contented,
　Her mesas and cañon-ways trod.
Then Dolores, the river of sorrow,
　Was a river of laughter and glee,
As she playfully dashed through the cañons
　In her turbulent rush to the sea.

High up on the cliffs in their dwellings,
  Which were apertures walled up with rocks,
Lived this people, sequestered and happy;
  Their dwellings now serve the wild fox.
They planted the maize and potato,
  The kind river caused them to grow,
So they worshipped the river with singing
  Which blent with its musical flow.

This people, so artless and peaceful,
  Knew nothing of carnage and war,
But dwelt in such quiet and plenty
  They knew not what weapons were for.
They gathered the maize in its season,
  Unmindful of famine or foe
And chanted their thanks to the spirits
  That dwelt in the cañons below.

But one evil day from the Northland
  Swept an army in battle array,
Which fell on this innocent people
  And massacred all in a day.
Their bodies were cast in the river,
  A feast for the vultures, when lo!
The laughter and song of the river
  Were changed to the wailing of woe.

Gone, gone are this people forever,
  Not a vestige nor remnant remains

To gather the maize in its season
  And join in the harvest refrains;
But the river still mourns for her people
  With weird and disconsolate flow,
Dolores, the river of sorrow,
  Dolores—the river of woe.

GREAT SHEPHERD OF THE COUNTLESS FLOCKS OF STARS

Great Shepherd of the countless flocks of stars,
  Which range the azure province of the sky,
Who marked the course for Jupiter and Mars,
  Nor leads the comet from its path awry;
    Though flaming constellations at Thy call
    Pass into being, or created, fall;
    Thou, who hast caused the firmament to be,
    In humbler pathways, Father, lead Thou me.

Thou, who hast framed the eagle's wing to soar
  Above the verdant prospects of the plain;
Whose law hath shaped the pebbles on the shore,
  The stately forests and the bearded grain;
    Whose hand hath formed the silvery satellite
    To shed her tender moonbeams o'er the night;
    Thou who hast placed the islands in the sea,
    With that same Wisdom, Father, lead Thou me.

THE RUINED CABIN

There's a pathos in the solemn desolation
  Of the mountain cabin sinking in decay,
With its threshold overgrown with vegetation,
  With its door unhinged and mouldering away.
There's a weird and most disconsolate expression
  In the sashless windows with their vacant stare,
As in mute appeal, or taciturn confession
  Of a wild and inconsolable despair.

With its ridgepole bent and broken in the centre,
  From its roof of dirt and weight of winter snows;
Where the only voice to greet you as you enter
    Is the wind which down the crumbling fireplace
        blows;
Where the chipmunk chatters in loquacious wonder,
  As unwonted steps invade his solitude;
Where the mountain rat secretes his varied plunder
  In the chimney corners, primitive and rude.

Where the spider spins his web in grim seclusion,
  To entrap the fly and vacillating moth;
From the rotten floor, in poisonous profusion
    Spring the toadstools, with their foul and fungous
        growth.
Void of symmetry and semblance of equation.

Through the chinkless cracks, the silvery moon
    and stars
And the sun, at each matutinal invasion,
  Shine as through a dismal dungeon's grated bars.

But no predatory hand in wanton malice
  Hath in vandal hour this dereliction wrought,
But the hand which crumbles pyramid and palace,
  The hand of Time with rust and ruin fraught;
Thus the proud or unpretentious habitation
  Shall succumb to age and melancholy mould;
All are subject to the same disintegration,
  For the occupant and house alike grow old.

AN IDYLL

I love to sit by the waterfall,
  And list to its laughing story,
As it fearlessly leaps o'er the rocky wall,
  From the mountain peaks stern and hoary;
Or watch the spray as the colors play,
  When the glorious sunlight kisses,
And tints confuse into rainbow hues
  To embellish the wild abysses.

I love the rose and the columbine,
  Whose delicate beauty pleases;
I love the breath of the fragrant pine,
  As it floats on the morning breezes;

I love the sound from the depths profound,
   When the Thunder-God is bringing
His crystal showers, to the tinted flowers,
   In their sweet profusion springing.

I love the lake in the mountain's lap;
   Without a flaw or error
Recording the clouds, which the peaks enwrap,
   And the trees, as a crystal mirror;
The wild delights of the mountain heights
   Thrill my breast with a keen devotion,
As songbirds love the blue arch above,
   Or the mariner loves the ocean.

THE BORDERLAND OF SLEEP

On the margin of the mystic shores of rest,
Where imagination mollifies the breast,
Where the fondest dreams their pleasant vigils keep,
In the vestibule of slumber, soft and deep,
Lies a neutral zone, salubrious and sweet,—
Where the realms of lethargy and action meet,—
      'Tis the borderland of sleep.

Here the halcyon delights float by and fade,
Or the evil visions hover and invade;
Here the bosom entertains its secret guest,
With the silent plaint of agony suppressed,

As unwelcome thoughts rise from the dust and
    mould,
Of the vanished years in pantomime unrolled,
            In this borderland of rest.

Neither wakeful, nor in sentient repose,
Nor in apathy, complete and comatose;
As when Lethe with her mild nepenthic surge,
Doth in chaos of forgetfulness submerge,
But a drowsy consciousness, a blend of dreams,
With reality's extravagant extremes;
            Such the zone on slumber's verge.

STELLAR NOCTURNE

Speeds the day in silent flight, on the sombre wings
        of night,
    As the dying sunlight glimmers in the west;
Soon the shadows cease to creep, for the sun has
        gone to sleep,
    And the scene is wrapped in somnolence and rest.

From a solitary star, in the realms of space afar,
    Faintly twinkling through the shadows of the
        night,
See the stellar force increased, till the scintillating
        east
    Seems a galaxy of constellations bright.

With its glittering display, see the gorgeous Milky
    Way,
  Which in twain the vaulted universe divides,
As the bridal veil serene of some fair celestial queen,
  Who, in jewelled state, o'er astral space presides.

All the heavens seem in tune, and the vacillating
    moon
  Bathes the landscape with her floods of silvery
    light;
Though the scenes of day are fair, naught in splen-
    dor can compare
  With the grandeur of the firmament at night.

FATHER, AT THY ALTAR KNEELING

Father, at Thy altar kneeling,
      Sin-defiled;
Seeking there the balm of healing,
To Thy Fatherhood appealing,
      See Thy child.

I am weary of transgressions;
      I have sinned;
Prone to vice and indiscretion,
Vacillation, misimpression,
      As the wind.

Neither sins nor imperfections
        I conceal;
Evil thoughts, impure reflections,
Faults in manifold directions,
        Can I feel.

I am tired of life's illusion,
        I would rest;
Leave its turmoil and confusion,
Fain would know the blest seclusion
        Of Thy breast.

Through the shadows of the valley
        As I speed,
Bid my faltering courage rally,
To resist each adverse sally;
        Wilt Thou lead?

For I know that Thou art reigning
        Over all;
With this confidence remaining,
Let me feel Thy Hand sustaining
        Lest I fall.

DREAMS

A dream is the ghost of a fond delight,
   An echo of former smiles or tears,
Wafted to us on the wings of night
   From the silent bourne of the vanished years.

A dream is a perished joy, restored
  From the mystical regions beyond our ken,
Which we fain would press as a thing adored,
  To our breasts, ere it fades and is lost again.

A dream is a buried hope exhumed,
  'Tis an iridescent thing of air,
Which mocks at the spirit, by fate entombed
  In the catacombs of a mute despair.

A dream is a reflex view of life,
  A blending of fancy with solemn truth,
A retrospection of mundane strife,
  Old age re-living the scenes of youth.

Our dreams are but mirrors for our desires;
  The proud ambition, the lofty aim
Achieved in our sleep, but the night expires
  And the dull existence plods on the same.

A dream is a feeble ray of light,
  A rift in the shadows through which we grope
An evidence that eternal night
  Can never extinguish the star of hope.

NOCTURNE

As fall the dews of slumber soft and deep,
  On wilderness and populated town,
Bound by the sweet influences of sleep,
  Proud reason abdicates her golden crown;

Dark Lethe, of oblivious renown,
Fain would I quaff from thy forgetful streams,
  In willing thralldom would I lay me down,
To court the fair companionship of dreams,
And bask within their iridescent beams.

Or linger in the vestibule of sleep,
  Where blow the winds of memory from the past,
Ere yet the languid shades of slumber deep
  Have o'er the sense their dormant shadows cast;
  Or muse upon the infinite and vast,
Till speculations various confuse,
  And thought, unmerciful iconoclast,
With shattered images the path bestrews,
Yet leads to chaos of conflicting views.

Now vanish all remembrance of the day,
  Complete immunity pervade the mind,
Let fond imagination hold her sway,
  With rule uncircumscribed and unconfined;
  Or soaring on the wings of fancy, wind
Through mystic realms of interstellar space,
  Where visions of supernal beauty bind
The drowsy consciousness in sweet embrace;
But dreamland fades, and morning comes apace.

THE TRUE FAITH

That faith is true whatever it may be,
  What ethics or traditions it may teach,
Whose whispers soothe the secret misery
  And mollify with soft, persuasive speech.

That faith is true that lightens pain and care,
  That false, which adds one burden to the load,
Whate'er its ornaments of psalm and prayer,
  A travesty on reason and on God.

That faith is true that buoys the sinking breast,
  When in the throes of some great agony,
That comforts the afflicted and distressed,
  And reconciles the trembling soul to die.

That faith is true that when the chilling blasts
  Of final dissolution overwhelm
Life's fragile bark, and shiver hull and masts,
  Sees but the hand of Love upon the helm.

A FRAGMENT

The bard who versifies for hire,
When no exalted thoughts inspire,
Tho' rhyme and metre be exact,
Conveys a sense of something lacked;
When moved by no poetic fire,
He twangs a dull and tuneless lyre.

MORTALITY

A Dissertation

"If a man die, shall he live again?"—Job xiv. 14.

Thou man of Uz,—
The query which thy fevered organs framed,
Unanswered still re-echoes in our ears.
Thy desolate interrogating cry,
Born of affliction, grievous and extreme,
Bridging the gulf of fleeting centuries,
Finds our weak tongues as impotent as thine,
To voice reply in accents void of doubt.
Though in our breasts awakening response,
'Tis but a repetition of thy plaint,
A faint reverberation of thy cry.
We peer into the darkness, but descry
Nor form, nor semblance, with our bootless gaze;
We call and list with ears attuned to hear;
No sound is wafted, and no glimmering ray
Breaks from that night, unlit by moon or star;
Nor gleam, nor spark, nor modicum of light
Is flashed from out the precincts of the tomb.

Death is the final principle of life,
The culmination of vicissitude,
The silent archer, whose unerring shaft
Doth pierce at last the most unyielding breast;
The reaper after whose fell harvesting,
No gleaner bends nor follows in his wake.

The gold of Ophir, and the pearls of Ind,
The sapphires and the rubies of the East,
Or all the treasures, which the fabled Gnomes,
In subterranean vaults and passages
Have guarded, multiplied by countless sums,
With Euclid's most exalted numeral
In computation, as the multiple
Of least proportion, for the passing breath
Can purchase neither respite nor reprieve,
Nor can prolong it, by one feeble gasp.

Nor fragrant balm, nor sweet preservative,
Nor caustic alkaloid, nor bitter herb
From Nature's various dispensary,
Elixir, lotion, nor restorative,
Nor prophylactic nor catholicon
Nor pharmacy's most potent stimulant
Can long retard the swift but viewless flight,
Of that mysterious thing we call the Soul.
Nor exorcism, nor the mystic power
Of incantation, nor of talisman,
Nor words of solemn theurgy pronounced,
Can break or dissipate that pallid spell;
Nor necromancy, nor phylactery,
Nor touch of magic wand, nor subtle force
Of conjuration, nor of sorcery, prevails
Against the shadows of the tomb;
Nor all the baleful arts of witchery,
Nor amulet withstand the charm of death.

Yea, man who rules the passive elements,
Enchaining them to service at his will,
Himself to death must yield obedience.
Yea, man who, through all disadvantages
And obstacles, has hewed his way aloft,
From out the labyrinth of ignorance,
Who sways the sceptre over conquered realms,
Of latent energy and unseen force,
Without condition or conceding term,
Surrenders to that sombre potentate.

Nor can in earth's remotest solitude,
In forest depths or undiscovered isle,
In dismal cavern or secretive cave
Escape the mandate of that grizzly King.
Nor wing of eagle, nor the fabled wings
Of hippogrif, of such velocity
As clothes the lightning and the thunderbolt,
Outstrip in speed the shadowy wings of death.

We pass along an ever-travelled road,
Worn by the silent and continuous tread
Of throngs innumerable, of every clime;
The countless generations of the past,
The uncomputed hosts and multitudes
Who trod the earth in ages most remote,
And those whose pale emaciated forms
The generous earth hath recently received,
The myriads of every race and tongue
Who have preceded us, have sent no word

Of cheer or comfort from that silent strand,
And no directions for our timorous steps.

Grim Dissolution knows no favorites,
But in his multiplicity of shapes
Invades alike, with stern resistless step,
The squalid hovel with its noisome air,
And palace most replete with opulence;
Those of exalted station, and the hordes
To whom existence means but servitude,
Who see the golden sun arise and bring
No intermission from their ceaseless toil,
Who hope for respite only with the night;
Those who in dread reluctance shrank from death,
And those who neither knew nor cared the hour,
To life and death alike indifferent,
Or fain themselves would snap the fragile thread;
Mankind in all conditions and degrees
Of culture, affluence and penury,
Of multiform endowments and desires,
With differing talents and proclivities,
Yea, all varieties and types of men,
With pathways various and diversified,
Have found their paths converging at the grave.

Each, as the gathering shadows of the night,
In solemn chaos of unfathomed gloom,
Descend in sombre, melancholy pall,
And mark apace life's transitory eve,
Must quaff, alike, the bitter draught of death,

The one libation in which all who breathe
May in all equity participate.
Each, at the expiration of his span,
Has found the same relentless terminal,
And faltering on dissolution's brink,
With what of strength, or guilt or innocence
Did mark the tenor of his brief career,
Has passed up to the margin of the grave,
Then disappeared forever.

What is Death?
We know not, yet in verity we feel
That, though of most immediate concern,
And shrouded deep in sable mystery,
Though most abstruse, intangible and strange,
'Tis not of our volition and control!
It therefore proves, as life doth ever prove,
With all abundant plenitude of proof,
A Force superior to human strength,
And should afford no premises for fear.

[FINIS]

Printed in the United States of America

"As stormy cowls their summits hid."

See page 19.

"Exceeding the tremendous height
Of brother peaks, on left and right."

See *page* 19.

"Beseamed with countless scars and rents
From combat with the elements."

See page 20.

"He towered with mute and massive form
A challenge to the gathering storm."

See page 20

"With swift and spoliating flow,
   Uprooting many a noble tree,
To strew the desert's waste below,
   With scattered drift-wood and debris."

See page 22.

141

"Arrayed in Nature's pristine dress
This was, indeed, a wilderness."

See page 29.

"We grew as two twin pines might grow,
  Upon the isolated edge,
Of some lone precipice or ledge."

See page 57.

143

"The noble spruce and stately fir
Stood draped in feathery garniture."

See page 119.

"From the mountain peaks crested with snow."

145

"High up on the cliffs in their dwellings,
   Which were apertures walled up with rocks,
Lived this people, sequestered and happy;
   Their dwellings now serve the wild fox."

See page 152.

"As it fearlessly leaps o'er the rocky wall
From the mountain peaks stern and hoary."

See page 124.

147

"I love the lake in the mountain's lap."

See page 125.